THE
LIGHT
OF REASON

THE
LIGHT
OF REASON

The Delight of the Awakened State

GLORIA EXCELSIOR

Copyright © 2014 Gloria Excelsior.

All rights reserved. No part of this book may be used or reproduced by any means, graphic, electronic, or mechanical, including photocopying, recording, taping or by any information storage retrieval system without the written permission of the publisher except in the case of brief quotations embodied in critical articles and reviews.

Balboa Press books may be ordered through booksellers or by contacting:

Balboa Press
A Division of Hay House
1663 Liberty Drive
Bloomington, IN 47403
www.balboapress.com
1 (877) 407-4847

Because of the dynamic nature of the Internet, any web addresses or links contained in this book may have changed since publication and may no longer be valid. The views expressed in this work are solely those of the author and do not necessarily reflect the views of the publisher, and the publisher hereby disclaims any responsibility for them.

The author of this book does not dispense medical advice or prescribe the use of any technique as a form of treatment for physical, emotional, or medical problems without the advice of a physician, either directly or indirectly. The intent of the author is only to offer information of a general nature to help you in your quest for emotional and spiritual well-being. In the event you use any of the information in this book for yourself, which is your constitutional right, the author and the publisher assume no responsibility for your actions.

Any people depicted in stock imagery provided by Thinkstock are models, and such images are being used for illustrative purposes only.
Certain stock imagery © Thinkstock.

Printed in the United States of America.

ISBN: 978-1-4525-2363-7 (sc)
ISBN: 978-1-4525-2365-1 (hc)
ISBN: 978-1-4525-2364-4 (e)

Library of Congress Control Number: 2014918417

Balboa Press rev. date: 10/23/14

To all loved ones who seek truth.

Contents

Book One

Remembering 2
Intention for the New Earth 4
The Potency of Recreative Elements 6
Finding Your Truth 9
Discovery of Reverence 11
Awakening to the Light of Reason 13
Day of Denial 14
New Healing Dynamics 17
We Are One 20

Book Two

The Potential of Light 22
The Veil of Linear Time 25
The Choice to Awaken 27
Healing Wisdom for Children 29
Unity of the Family 32
Conditions within the Factor of Convenience 33
Healing Light of Guidance 35
World Leadership of Service 36
Birthing Process of the New Earth 39
The Fold of Love and Choice of Action 41
Commitment and Conditions 43

Book Three

Commitment for the Earth's Survival 48
Forgiveness and the Test of Love 50
The Gift of the Fifth Dimension 52

New Healing Solutions 54
The Evolutionary Pathway 57
Changes 59
The Divine Light of Existence 61
You Are Holy 63
Process of Self-reflection 65
The Awakened Ones 68
Power of Forgiveness 72
The Contract of the Soul 75

Book Four

The Thriving of the New Earth 80
Healing Elements Called Manifestations 84
The Experience of Conscious Awareness 85
Moving Into Balance 88
The Lotus of Grace 91
Love Elements of Consciousness 93
Holy Redemption 95

Book Five

The Now Is in the Present 98
What You Think, You Create 100
Presence and Worthiness 102
The Abiding of Universal Laws 104
The Universal Law of Intention 105
The Universal Law of Commitment 108
The Universal Law of Pleasure 109
The Universal Law of Duality 111
The Masters of the Light Decree a Miracle of Movement 113
The Bond of Light Forces 117
Welcome Home 120
A New World Order 122
The Expression of the Enlightened State 124

Book Six

Codes of Worth 128
Light and Dark Elements 130
Crossroads of Desire 134
Meet Your True Self... 136
The Pretender, Called the Shadow 140

Book Seven

The Breaking of Chains... 144
Divine Planning..147
Meeting Challenges with Fortitude................................149
The Adventure 151
Afterword 155
Glossary.. 157

May this light, pure and strong, traverse this great planet, weaving its hope into the hearts of all those who receive.

Book One

A New Dawn of Reason

Remembering

Every little drop of water is of thy countenance.

Every intake of breath is the wind's breath of desire.

Every thunderstorm is a call for nature to love.

Every relationship on this planet is the challenge of the Lord thy God.

Every partnership within this challenge is not about the other's worthiness.

Every challenge within partnership is a call to awaken the self to inner knowing.

Every condition within the partnership is the worthiness of desire to search out God.

The relationship with the self is the relationship with God.

God is within the relationship.

God is the worthiness.

God is the partnership.

There was a time when all was dark. There was no light. During this time of nothing, elements of our making were at play.

We, the light, provided for the thoughts and deeds to manifest as they should. This was our manifesto of life. Through this arrangement, we were provided many opportunities to create.

Within these creative elements, we were able to challenge the darkness. This challenge was one of intensity and ferociousness, where there was much drama and then exhilaration. The darkness was removed in partiality and became a fixed day. The fixed day is what the Earth is experiencing at this moment, in this period of time.

When this was accomplished, we designed another manifestation. We challenged the darkness and gained more awareness for the light that shone. This awareness was in the form of living elements. As these living elements gained in strength, we knew that there should be a favored addition to this light.

This addition was the bonding and reflection of ourselves in our likeness. We have been well pleased and have appreciated the worthiness of each and every soul on this Earth. This has been our nature and our passion. This has been our investment in manifestation outcomes from the beginning of time.

It is important for the Gloria and the Lord thy God to share again the beginnings of the story of creation, from a deeper perspective of understanding for the beings on this Earth who are ready in their evolutionary journey to hear of this tale. With this disclosure, we will be able to move forward into the concepts to be presented in the form of recreation elements for the new Earth reality.

Intention for the New Earth

This book is full of intention. The words in each phrase, each sentence, each paragraph, and each page are infused with light and love from the Lord thy God speaking with directness to all who are willing to attend to these teachings. Paired with these words are the words of Gloria, who is beside the Lord as he speaks. The Gloria conveys a message full of admiration for all who read this document.

The message from the Lord thy God is here. It is in the now. It is written by the one who is within the embrace of the Almighty who thrives with her presence. This light being has been created for the new coming to this Earth that will be called recreation. With this coming will be a new earthly understanding and a strong, dynamic connection with the power of light.

This being is full of glory, for she holds great wealth for all of mankind and for those who have passed from this earthly realm. You see, dear ones, the Gloria is here to manifest the connecting of heaven and Earth in a way that has never been envisioned in all of Earth's history.

The connection between these two realms will enrich all who partake in this classical, yet grand experience. There will also be a stripping of the veil of denial which will end the deception of a reality that does not exist and has never existed.

The stripping of this veil will end the conjecture of false thought and false action of all on this planet. This conjecture is causing pain, sorrow, and discomfort throughout this world. The time has come for this veil of misinformation to be lifted for all of eternity. Only the new Earth reality will remain.

The Light of Reason

This is not the end of the world; it is a beginning. It is a renewal that will prove to be profound in nature and in all human elements of existence. All living elements will thrive with the intention of the one who will be the guiding light to all who agree to accept this condition of worthiness.

She is your example. She is your guide. She shares your experiences. She knows of your pain, sorrows, turmoil. She knows of your wisdom and of your light. There is no veil between the Gloria and your countenance. There is no veil between Gloria and the Lord thy God.

Gloria is the bonding, the union, the love that is extended from on high to all living beings on this earthly plane. Gloria carries light forward. She exudes this light for the well-being of all of mankind; it is the healing element for all of nature and everything on this planet. It is time for this healing. It is time for a rearrangement from Source. It is time for the veil to be lifted.

The Potency of Recreative Elements

THE LORD IS WELL pleased because the Earth is within recreation. These creative elements will extinguish the drive for unworthiness, self-loathing, and judgment of the self and of the other. This recreation of the planet will move all forward into a new Earth full of vibrant energy that will sustain and balance this planet.

The task is not daunting. The conditions will not be difficult. The challenges of correction will be representative of honoring this planet in all aspects of commitment to the other.

The other will be of prime consideration: the other who suffers, condemns, judges, and denies God; the other who challenges all aspects of love and disregards all interest in caring for beings on this planet; this other is being challenged by the Lord thy God, the Almighty, who is present and swift of action. The challenge is not to be feared but revered. The challenge of the Lord thy God is one of service.

Serve the Lord thy God through service for the other. Serve the ones who are in need in thy Name. Serve all within relationship with honor and openness.

Open your heart to the joys of everyday existence, knowing that you are loved and honored by all divine elements.

Your service will be known. The service will be a call for you to participate in this healing of the new Earth as it begins to unfold.

The elements of change are upon each one of you who participates in this beautiful healing process given by the one called Gloria, my beloved.

This is not an offer. This is a clear understanding of intent being projected to Earth from the Lord thy God. Those who reject the conditions set on these pages will not be part of the new world order. There will be a day of judgment. Each one will be challenged by the Lord thy God who will sit in judgment for unworthy deeds.

There will be an accounting of deeds that hold darkness and do not hold the light of love.

There will be an accounting of deeds that hold lack of forgiveness for the self and others.

There will be an accounting of deeds that hold a lack of compassion where one has stepped over another in need.

There will be an accounting of deeds of betrayal, deceit, and denial of personal truth.

It is time to step forward into a new dawn of reason. It is time to put away or be done with the deeds of the past and view existence with a sense of presence.

This, dear ones, is the awakening for which so many on this planet have been praying. This is the awakening to new possibilities. This is the awakening into love for all fellow beings on this Earth. This is the awakening of all living things that will begin to thrive within a balanced and healing Earth environment. Each have a choice to believe or ignore the fact that:

God is benevolent.
God listens.
God speaks.

Gloria Excelsior

God is here.
This is your blessing.
This is your nature.
This is your choice.

All have a choice: acceptance of love, light, laughter, and healing or the acceptance of a darkness devoid of all of these elements offered in the name of Gloria.

Dear ones, it is time for a commitment of your worthiness. This worthiness is well established by heavenly order. It is your responsibility to move into the understanding of who you are.

You are the light, the stars, and the breath of the wind. You are the waves lapping on a sandy shore. You are a reflection of love, laughter and of memories that have already occurred. You are all of these thoughts, all of these actions.

How is perfection expressed? This perfection is of creative elements. This perfection is of the divine who deeply loves and cherishes each one of you.

The light that you carry merges with the others around you. There is no division and no end. This light conveys the wealth of the universal energy that feeds and nurtures your being.

This wealth brings forth responsibility for your worthiness on this new earthly plane of existence.

Finding Your Truth

THIS RESPONSIBILITY IS A reflection of your personal truth. It is not an easy task to find your truth. Truth is hidden under many layers of denial of what is the real truth. Denial stands in the way of your courage to look beyond discomfort and to challenge a stronger look at personal strengths. The challenge is to find the strength of your own truth.

Finding the structure of your truth is not the same as seeing the conditions of your beliefs. Belief is very different from truth. The truth of self is the heart of the matter. The self is your truth. The self is your true essence of being. The self holds the key to your personal truth. The self is called your soul. This is the soul of life, of your truth. Your soul holds the truth within. The soul only knows the deep truth of the self.

With this knowledge comes love—the love of truth. Through this personal truth, the love of God is born. The love for thy God on high exists in pure form within this strength of truth. This is the truth of divine elements, creation, and universal love for all living things. You are this truth. You are this perfection of being. You are a child of God. You are a reflection of the Almighty, the all, the one. You are all of that.

Wherefore I say unto you, in the name of the Lord thy God, the time has come to look within the self. Consider the seeing with a naked eye of intent. Use this intent to search and find the true essence of your being. With this search will be many gifts offered from on high. These gifts will be in the form of joy, comfort, consideration, and assurance of well-being that will shape a new vision of worthiness. The final gift from this self-reflection will be the ability to truly feel the love of your God who delights in the revelation of truth. Your God shares this awakening time with you, and with this awakening, the truth becomes the way, the light, and the reason for being on this planet called the new Earth.

The conditions of this planet need your assistance. The assistance cannot be claimed by a group or an institution or a consortium. You must respond to this earthly distress and be the active participant who will take ownership for all of your future actions and development.

This action will be in the form of your personal truth. An alignment exists between your truth and of God's knowing. Action will be taken with personal integrity matching your truth.

The action is one of confirmation of the love one will hold for the other, the action of a confirmation of all living things on this planet where all healing possibilities reside.

The healing of the plants and animals in the kingdom of life requires your support.

This will be your truth. This is the truth of loving life, the life of the other who claims truth.

Seeking truth is not an easy subject to convey to those who struggle with denial and who see through a myopic lens of distortion: This impaired vision results in regrets about old patterns of behaviors, want of resourcefulness, and a return to old ways of disregard and destruction of this earthly realm.

For some, this will be the ultimate challenge: to meet the conditions of the Lord thy God in matters of natural endeavors that must be nurtured by each individual seeking the truth.

Discovery of Reverence

THIS CLAIM TO THE truth will be in the form of reverence. Reverence through truth reflects love for this Earth. This truth holds reverence for the ancestors who created for everyone on this Earth. This truth holds reverence for the unborn who will seed this new Earth and bring forward untold wealth and healing through new technological developments. They will support Earth to a new threshold of reverence for all living things.

It will come to pass that all beings on this new Earth will be struck with a sense of wonder. This wonder will signal the start of the changes for the Lord on high to manifest before the population of this earthly realm. The manifestation will be complete and inevitable.

This manifestation will touch the hearts and minds of each living being. The understanding of forgiveness will be convincing and dramatized for all to see and experience. Self-forgiveness will unfold with tears of gladness and renewal. The re-new-all will tear down the barriers between time and space. This space/time continuum will encompass all healing elements. The production of wealth will begin to manifest in the form of creative manifestations of the true self—the soul of eternal life. This life force will begin to unfold within and will challenge old behaviors and past lessons.

The lessons of old will be counted. The accounting will begin with a powerful force of love that will exude, emanate, and coalesce within each entity of this earthly state. Each entity will experience gratitude for this task of reflection. Each one will begin to see the light of reason—the message from the Lord thy God. Each individual will see these lessons in full light and come to realize that all has been forgiven.

This forgiveness will become a profound awareness. This awareness is not to be dismissed or minimized. It is a communication of love and endearment; it also holds a challenge. This challenge will be called a waking up or an awakening of the spirit of each soul.

Awakening to the Light of Reason

THIS AWAKENING PROCESS IS the beginning of your personal evolution into the mainstream of a richness that is beyond your comprehension. It is the richness of life; the richness of love, and the richness of the truth of self.

This truth reflects and moves into a wealth of relationships that will build firm structures of intense belonging for all who partake in this beautiful discovery.

Yes, some will not be able to accept this wealth of love and forgiveness. This lack will manifest as well. It will become clear to them that the time of this wealth is not upon them. It will become clear that they will not be a part of this experience of the new conditions set forth for the healing changes for others. This awareness will be an awakening to the realization that the time and space continuum will not be upon their countenance, and there will be a denial of forgiveness from on high.

Day of Denial

THIS WILL BE THE event called judgment day. This is the day of denial of the Lord thy God. This is the day when it will be the right of each person to deny the essence of the divinity and to move away from the light of reason.

There will be no blame. There will be no recrimination. There will be nothing for these people to do. The doing is done. The choice of conditions has been met by the denial of love and light and the denial of reverence for the other. The other is a reflection of nothing shared. There is no wealth within the conditions, but only recrimination. There is no relating to healing elements infused with love. There is only a hatred for the self and a hatred for others. Hate does not hold light. It is an eternal place that only absorbs blackness. This darkness is not of the new earthly experience.

Wherefore I say unto you, the choice is yours to make. The light of reason is upon you. The light of forgiveness is yours to behold. The light of your countenance shines. Take this love. Take this light.

Take this challenge; move into the light of acceptance, gratitude, and awareness of the abundance of this new earthly realm that exudes God's love for you. Awaken to the coming of the Lord.

With this intention will be the peril of self-contradiction. Within each and every one of you will be a small voice crying with discomfort, a similar voice that will call out with fear and resistance, and a louder voice within that will counsel you to make choices full of ease and comfort.

These voices, held within, are the voices of personal peril. These voices are the voices that will speak of doom, woe, and lack of credibility of Source, your divine, guiding light. These voices are not your truth. The voices are not the light and the way; they consist of other forces dimming your light and love. They are the voices that carry you down the path into darkness.

Be aware of these challenging voices. Be aware of their power to simultaneously corrupt and carry you away from your true guidance—your truth of following the Lord thy God into the light.

The guidelines are simple for you to understand. Following these instructions will help you to find your personal strength and to move into the light of reason—the reason for your being.

Your being is of great strength, character, and compassion for all of the light beings on this new Earth.

The measure of the challenges will come from the Lord thy God on high. This measure is not yours. It is the measure of all of your history from the beginning of creation. The divine is aware of your measure, the measure of deeds that have been accomplished. This measure is of life conditions claimed and the measure of your choices since the inception of time.

The accounting has been completed. The door has been opened for you to step through the threshold of light and love and to begin in earnest the changes that will sweep you forward into a wealth of indescribable magnitude.

Some will describe this stepping through the threshold as an entry into the heavenly realm. Some will describe it as entering a city of gold, with riches beyond compare. Some will cry foul and say there is a luring element full of mistrust and deceit.

Gloria Excelsior

This threshold is a metaphor. The metaphor is about stepping forward into your truth. When one has the courage to walk through this challenging gate to find the truth, one is moved into a state of well-being, honor, compassion, and trustworthiness. This state of trustworthiness is the equivalent of a state of peacefulness, clarity, and delight. It is a heavenly state of being.

Wherefore I say unto you, now is the time to move forward into a state of well-being, a state of heavenly peace, where all will express their truth, their ideas, and their goodwill so that others will be able to express their own vital truth. This forum of expression will be the basis for a broad, expressive, open dialogue between all who move through this threshold into the truth of the light of reason.

The pattern of denial is strong. It has been a contention with the Lord thy God. This pattern is a creation of the past to cover past deeds. Denial is like a cloud that obscures the sky. It blocks the truth. It reduces clarity. It creates a sense of forgetting. Denial is the forgetting of past deeds and experiences. Denial rewards this forgetting with repetitive outcomes affecting the worthiness within each being of light.

This worthiness is denied. It is shadowed by the cloud of denial. It is a conditioned response that is not needed during this evolutionary phase of human beings' existence. Denial is not useful. It is not purposeful; therefore, it will be abolished by the Lord who reigns.

It is done.

Wherefore I say unto you, the truth is your reality. The truth is your light. There is no shadow that covers your truth, for you are the light of God. Your countenance shines with brilliance. You are well loved and guided by the light of your soul that holds the truth of your nature.

New Healing Dynamics

The elements of change are upon us. There will be a change of dynamics moving forward to engage in healing structures. These healing structures are designed to assist in all healing endeavors on this new Earth. These teachings will address the new healing dynamics that will manifest for the wealth and health of all on this planet. These healing elements will be called forth by the one called Gloria. The Gloria is the mother of all of creation and she represents all healing elements.

Consideration of all living things is of the utmost importance. The well-being of all living things is an imperative aspect of love and truth, held deeply in the form of the Gloria Excelsior. She holds the truth of each of you who suffers from untold hardships through illness. She grieves in her heart when her people are suffering.

Gloria is your mother. The Lord thy God is your father, and we are content in moving our people to a place of worthiness and well-being. It will be a healing zone for all. This is the time and space for disease to be no more. This is the time and space for everyone to experience the body in a way that has never been seen before. The experience of well-being, in a body that now holds intense light, will move with loving tenderness through all bodily structures with a healing cadence of goodwill from on high. This is representative of the mother of forgiveness, of delight, and the light of compassion.

The mother of goodness, purity, and light is the guidance that is required on this planet. This healing endeavor demonstrates this honoring of the all who inhabit this planet of beauty. The beauty is exemplified by all who choose to make the new Earth their home, filled with love and compassion for the other within the experience of relationship. This is the glorification of the one who has claim on the emancipation of all who participate in this grand healing event bringing the Earth into balance. This is the balance of love, understanding, worthiness, and above all, gratitude to be expressed to mother Earth, the provider of all earthly goods.

Gloria (the mother of creation) and the Earth (the mother of Provision) respectfully regard life as a point of light which needs to be fully nurtured. Therefore, the mothers are ready to join together to move into creative energy for healing endeavors. Gloria will represent the physicality of mother Earth and exemplify all that is on this earthly plane called the new Earth. Together, there will be majesty in the projection that creates light and love through all things on this planet.

This experience will move creation to a new level of form and action. All will participate in this moving experience as it unfolds.

Mother Earth desires specific considerations from the people of the new Earth. These considerations will prove to be inventive in nature. They will employ technology primarily to create a healthy planet. The Earth is in peril. There is no judgment from mother Earth. The justice of conditions will be met by the Lord thy God and will not be the responsibility of mother Earth who has born the suffering with grace and persistence in protection of the planet's environment. Protection through earthly measures is not needed in this point of evolutionary progress.

Technological advancements will become the key factors of healing. Yes, there will be initial limitations on converting the old technology to new technological advancements. The transition will be calculated in such a way that the changes will exemplify a world becoming plentiful versus a world suffering from loss of resources, clean air, fertile soil and, above all, the loss of plentiful water.

The advancement of these programs will be created and distributed in the form of knowledge within future scientific endeavors. The flux of information will feed the network of resources in hydraulics, response engineering, and all fields of science, including aerodynamics.

The Lord thy God will call forth learned individuals to move together as one to manifest and implement safety guidelines for all earthly endeavors. These will sustain and develop a healthy and thriving new Earth system. The interactions of all living forces will thrive as one, supporting all beings on this planet called the new Earth.

Wherefore I say unto you, be still. Be aware of all living organisms on this beautiful system of a planet. Honor and revere all systems with love and light. Revere the Lord and all the actions that will be taken from this moment forward. The Lord protects the earthly environment and keeps it safe from harm. The Lord honors all things possible and supports Gloria and all earthly healing elements with love and gratitude for the conditions of repair and constructive changes occurring through the intent of Gloria on high.

We Are One

THE AWARENESS OF ALL living entities is a matter of trusting the changes that will be manifested. Some of the manifestations will be of a kind where the distinction between living and non-living will be difficult to determine. Becoming aware of this lack of distinction will be the next lesson in understanding.

All objects in this plane of existence hold immense power and honor for each other. With this new development in understanding, the Earth's future will be complete. The Earth and every particle therein is a manifestation of the Lord thy God. Everything is that. The Lord thy God lives and breathes in, around, and through this universal field and thrives on this experience of existence.

This is the way, the light, the passion of being. The Lord thy God lives through your existence, your passion, and your love for those you honor and care for. In all this service, you are honoring the Lord who thrives within this field of love and who creates heavenly bodies around this beautiful, vibrant place called Earth. This is the new Earth of God's passion and delight.

Wherefore I say unto you, see the light of reason. This is the reason for your being: delighting in the essence of Almighty God and thriving in an environment that enfolds all in an embrace of a world without end.

Book Two

*The Expression of
Love and Light*

The Potential of Light

Every possibility is within reach. The conditions on this Earth are met, and the Lord is well pleased with the results. All is appropriate for this time and for this space.

The conditions of service are being measured through notation and development. The development will include all species on this planet. The creative elements are forming bonds between the richest and poorest of all universal elements. This bonding will form a new attachment to the all within the cosmos of reason.

The cosmos needs support from all who comply with these teachings. The cosmos is charged with the expression of love and light to all reaches of universality. The light is charged with specific energy fields creating a field of vision that shall become a wondrous sight for the human race.

This light will manifest visual results for all living and non-living entities in and among this galaxy and beyond, even into the infinite universe.

This light penetrates the darkest fields that impose a fear-based union on those who experience the discomfort of unknowing.

This light brings about an unavoidable change in dynamic.

This light creates.

This light infuses the total potential within each molecular, neutronic component existing in the universal field of energetic forces. This gravitational pull is the dynamic of experience on this planet called Earth.

The changes that are gifted by divine light will be multifaceted. They will be profound and swift in nature and will reflect the power and glory of divine outcomes.

Whenever dynamic changes occur, there is a reaction to the outcome of equal proportion. This outcome is a notation from Source, your divine, who manifests this condition.

All conditions created are for the measurement of global unity of the Earth's health. These measurements reflect the healing potential exuded from the Earth's field of energy. This measurement is a value not yet understood by technological aspects within the framework of known scientific relativity awareness.

The deepening of understanding will be brought forth by individuals who will be called by divine elements to respond to this new phase of investigative research on dynamism. It will affect all future understandings of mobility for the Earth and those areas beyond the Earth's gravitational pull.

These responses to pull will be in the form of gastroentro harnessing. This harnessing of the energy from the Earth's core will triangulate with the redistribution factors that are held by divine light of intention.

This intention will catapult the Earth out of its orbit and into another strategic place within this solar system. The planet will be better suited for this placement and will thrive in all areas of well-being.

Nature will thrive and become plentiful.

Gloria Excelsior

The natural order of all living entities will become balanced, and species will no longer be at risk.

The Earth will function at a faster rate when one calculates day and night. The rate will change the value of all time elements and systems. The value of time will move from linear to a multi-track system, where all will have the ability to navigate between the past and future.

The Veil of Linear Time

WITH THESE CHANGES, THERE will be a cry of freedom to move from one reality to another. There will be no barrier between those who have passed and those who are coming to this Earth. There will be the freedom to be surrounded by loved ones from the past and the future, loved ones who call out your name with blessings of love.

This will be a discovery of a love not understood before. It will be a well of completeness filling the space of loneliness for those who have passed through the door of distance between themselves and you. They have remained complete but have been behind this veil of linear time. This veil will be lifted with purposefulness and delight.

The Lord thy God has spoken:

Wherefore I say unto you, rejoice, for this will be the day when all will experience the freedom of being in the light of reason. This light of reason holds the value of time in a way that opens the gates between heaven and Earth. This will be the experience of heaven on Earth's soil. It will be done in your name, for your sake, and for the honoring bestowed on the Lord thy God, the God who cherishes all relationships and who loves all his children.

It is written by my beloved Gloria that all of this will unfold within your lifespan of Earth time. I say unto you, rejoice. There is eternal life that has no beginning and no end.

There is a misnomer regarding this basic tenet. The misunderstanding is one that needs clarifying. There is no death. There is only life. This life is full and vibrant. This life will be matched with perceivable past and future experiences. These experiences will be provided for you with the opportunities of service to the other. There will be much to do and many to serve within this understanding and framework of time.

The Choice to Awaken

THE TIME HAS COME to experience life fully in the way it was intended. The beings on this planet are in a position to choose service to all divine elements within the range of love and light. There is also a choice to move away from the light of reason and into a darkness that diminishes the needs of others and the judgment of the conditions of the Lord thy God who honors this light of reason.

The choice will have a ring of assurance and clarity for you and your understanding. This choice will be your call and will be honored.

The miracle of this production creates a worthy choice. All are worthy to produce a wealth of choices to suit their needs. These needs are for the enhancement of one's own spirit, the feeding of one's passion, and the continual service requirements within all relational bonds.

These choices are the basis for the wealth of the individual and the wealth of others who receive the sharing from the choices made in the name of the Lord and in the name of love.

These choices will proclaim the Lord on high as the father of freedom. There is the freedom to be and the freedom to experience salvation.

There is the freedom to explore the true potential of all living entities within a thriving sense of well-being and lack of want. All of these things are possible within the boundaries of learning and valuing a deeper love of life for the benefit of all. This will be the beginning of a world without end.

Gloria Excelsior

Challenges will be met with creative solutions. Organizations will form to give direction to those who are in need of service. Industry will serve the new living requirement demands of all who will move into the accommodations they desire. Areas of production will serve the people's needs with mindful caring for the tenderness that mother Earth deserves.

Healing Wisdom for Children

THE CHILDREN WILL BE fed, clothed, and sheltered with an honor that is endearing to and respectful of their tender hearts. There will be abundance; it will be full of a complete state of union with divine elements infused with light.

The coming of this light of reason is needed by all little ones who suffer on this planet. The Gloria pines for the truth to appear to all who wish to see a solution to the plight of these beautiful souls crying out with dignity, but are not yet fed. These little ones call for the love they deserve from others, but they are not heard. The Gloria Excelsior weeps for their lost potential through limitations dictated by others. She knows each and every distressful moment these little ones suffer.

The suffering begins as a seed during the conception process, and as this seedling develops, so does the potential of the self.

The self is creation. The self is the understanding. The self is the beginning of worthiness in the womb of the mother. The self senses all, feels all, hears all, and through these senses, sees all. The child of God is held and cherished in the arms of the Lord thy God.

This time of growth and change is experienced in condensed time where, within the darkness of the womb, life takes on meaning—the meaning of worthiness.

Each growing life in utero knows that the experience of God's love is strong and good. Each life knows and experiences the self, which is full of unwritten potential. As development progresses, each soul begins to be aware of the cadence of being with their chosen family members.

The sharing of emotions between these family members is complete and memorable. These memories are stored inside each child in development. The storage of these experiences unfolds in the value of each child's expression of worthiness.

The essence of this explanation is clear. The Gloria will have no more of this. The Gloria will be moving forward with great healing potential to recreate a design of healing wisdom whereby each child, from this point forward, will be under her protection and light.

Each child will be shown reverence and comfort and will experience the delight of many lessons to be learned on this earthly plane called the new Earth.

Each child will be guided by the light of reason. This light will be the impetus for the potential worth of each child to be expressed clearly and completely within the embrace of beloved family members who love, honor, and obey this treatise and who commit to fully support new life.

There will be no want. Needs will be met. No conditions will be harmful to those in uteri.

There will be no challenges as to the worthiness of this new life.

There will be a firm commitment to life and love between all parties.

There will be a strong connection between mother and child.

There will be a strengthening bond between children within the household, where the bonds will unfold with reverence for each other.

This is the treatise of agreement for all to participate. This is the agreement that is clarified by the Gloria of delight who knows.

It is done.

The satisfaction of the Lord thy God is complete in this understanding.

Unity of the Family

THESE GUIDELINES ARE NEEDED to move forth into unity, the unity of the family. Understanding the importance of the role of this unit within the new society will hold reverence for all, from the very young to the very seasoned. As this regard matures, there will be a deeper commitment to gender equality within each unit, gaining strength under the guidance of the union between Gloria and the Lord thy God.

This unit cannot be broken. This union of divine intelligence was created for the perfection of the light of all beings on this beautiful Earth. Within this union, there is no division of self. There is only continuance of the other. The union is complete, and we are satisfied with our role in service to you, our people of worth.

Let it be known that within the union, respect will reign. The respect for the other gender will be steadfast. Within all unions will be a merging at the soul level, where the final commitment will be met with eternal reverence to divine elements of creation.

Conditions within the Factor of Convenience

WITHIN THIS ARRANGEMENT AT the soul level, a factor must be considered: the factor of convenience. This factor states that convenience will be considered for the other. This convenience will be a demonstration of a loving, caring way of being within the merging of the two souls in marriage. The marriage of convenience shall be one of bonding, merging, and committing that goes beyond sexual needs. The merging will extend to a rich relationship, full of transitions from one deep love to further deepening of the expression of love within the inner guidance of each bonded partner. This inner guidance will carry the load of love and light and challenge both individuals to create opportunities for growth within the marriage.

It is the condition of all beings to be responsive to each other in all types of communication. There will be no more doubt, no more loneliness, and no more lack within the partnership. This partnership will swell with admiration for the other. Gratitude and harmony will be the key to unlocking the heart's desire.

Unlocking the heart will serve to free the true essence of your being. It will bring forth your light to attend to the truth of who you are, and you will view the truth of your potential within the social structure of the new Earth.

Trust is the measure of the relationship one has with the Lord thy God. Trust is the condition that will move the one on the new Earth into the condition of the fifth element changes. These

Gloria Excelsior

changes represent a new space in time called the fifth dimension. Your guidance will be the key. Your trust will be the key. This is the way, this is the light, and this is the condition.

The first condition is trust.

Treat is the second condition. Treat others with the tenderness of a newborn. Treat others with the skill of a trained physician who cares for the human body with compassion and integrity.

The third condition is to welcome all toward the light.

The fourth condition is to sweep the heart clean of all unnecessary hurts and regrets.

The fifth condition is to love beyond all reason, for this, too, relates to trusting the Lord thy God, who loves beyond all measure.

Wherefore I say unto you, rejoice! The new Earth is in the making. The new Earth is in the being. The new Earth is within creative elements and will be moving to the threshold of existence.

Healing Light of Guidance

THROUGH THIS NEW EXISTENCE, there will be healing light, the kind of healing light that has never existed in memory. This healing light manifests from the one who knows, the glory, the glorious, the avatar who has come to this Earth to guide you to safety. The Gloria will guide you to the Lord thy God. She will direct all who answer the call of truth.

Trust in the Lord, and have the courage to move into the light of reason with the fundamental security that she will be providing her guiding light of reality. This is the provision for you. This is your safe travel within the awakening to a new reality. This is the reality of the new Earth.

Take her hand, and trust that you are well cared for. Take her hand, and she will lead with kindness for all. Take her hand, and move into acceptance that you are worthy. Take her hand, and you will be well looked after. She is your avatar who is all powerful. She knows. She is one with the all. She is one with Source. She is all of that.

In praise for the Gloria who will bring God's lambs into safety. In praise for Gloria who will bring this Earth into balance. In praise for Gloria who honors the all with integrity and the power of light and love. In praise of the power that exudes God's presence in all things eternal.

This is the mandate that has been given to the one called Gloria. She sits in full honor with the Lord thy God as his consort. Gloria is the feminine of divinity. She is my light. She is my love. She is the understanding of us both and conveys all things to you, my people, her people of wealth and beauty.

World Leadership of Service

THE HEAVENLY HOSTS PRAISE this venture. This venture is purposeful and needed for the purification of all who participate in this construction of the new Earth consortium of world order. This world order is the mainstay of our existence and will meet challenges with openness, transparency, and integrity of the highest order.

This world leadership will form a government for the people and be transparent before the people who produce for the well-being of others. This government will provide the organizational consistencies to support the all within the social base of the new Earth.

Each section or appendage of this government will move independently to provide direct service when specific needs arise. Independence is the key to these support systems. These independent agencies will move like outreach programs to sort out problems and difficulties within their area of service. Through this response method, the service will be direct, active, and effective.

The supervision of all outreach governmental agencies will be moved to areas that are accessible to outreach workers. These workers will be the voice and the bond with the people and communities in need of assistance. The assistance will be direct and swift. Embedded within the service will be the pleasure of the experience of helping others in need.

This sense of gratitude will be treasured by all, and the wheel of this service will extend outward, as one might envision spokes in a wheel of a simple bicycle. When one receives service, whether it is in the form of provision, housing, or support systems, it will be expected that service will move forward to another. As one receives, one becomes sustained and moves into balance as a healing outcome. With these improvements, and when ready, those who have been served will begin to serve as well.

This service will form a chain of gratitude that will begin to link the new Earth in a way never before seen. There will be no barriers to receiving gratitude. There will be no conclusions of judgment. There will be only compassion for the other, who will receive personal sustenance.

There will be times of adjustment, and challenges will seem insurmountable. There will be moments of clarity allowing a vision or a knowing of a certain pathway to create for better organizational tools and motivations.

Government formation will be structured around the economy, ergonomics, dynamic medicine, commerce, planetary guidance, dynamic engineering, academic growth, technological construction, healing chamber health, social support systems, planet sustainability, outreach and services, ancestry support systems, and people's forums.

Within these units of governmental agencies, flags of service will fly high for all to see. Contractual agreements will be offered to the finest minds open to creative ideas and unafraid of meeting new challenges, new experiences, and new ways of collaboration. These individuals with like minds and diverse ideas will directly address specific planetary issues, focusing on balancing all aspects of worthiness dynamics that surround the Earth in truth and light. These dynamics will be the priority of all healing outcomes, and each governmental agency will be charged with this mandate.

Gloria Excelsior

This is the time when Gloria will engage in many manifestations of consequence to universal elements. It is with these developments that the changes for the Earth will progress into bold action, righting the imbalances that have accumulated over many lifetimes. These changes will form a bond between mother Earth and the cosmos. This is the unfurling of potential that has been discussed. This is the dynamic that will ensure that the new Earth will receive the wealth that it deserves.

Let it be done with the magnitude of deservedness. Let it be done in the name of thy heavenly Father who loves and cares for this special planet called Earth. This magnitude is the gift of discovery to the inhabitants of this world. A new world order will be created.

Birthing Process of the New Earth

The new Earth is born. This birthing process will be of short duration. It will be swift and difficult and will manifest outcomes beyond human comprehension. Attuning to this light process, Gloria will be the catalyst of forward movement for this birthing process.

The worthiness of this one called Gloria is beyond the comprehension of the cosmos of knowing. The glory of divinity shines with the intensity of white light. This light calls forth all within the cosmos to coalesce and be with the Gloria on high who is the savior of Earth.

She is the feminine of Jesus Christ. She is the Christ who loves and forgives. She is that.

She represents the Father. She is the daughter, and she is the Holy Ghost.

This woman of Christ shares this role with him. They walk together in divine light. They share all worldly tasks together. They love all living entities within this setting called the new Earth.

In early times, Christ the Lord died. This was always the plan, dear ones. Jesus Christ gave up his life to move everyone forward into the light of the Lord thy God. All of this was ordained, and it was good.

The Gloria is here by my, the Lord thy God's direction. She is the representative of this next phase of your development. She will be the direction, the light, the reason. She will lead her people out of chaos and into the light of reason.

It is done.

It is done in the name of the Lord thy God who rules all universal existence and beyond with the eternal light of gratitude.

The knowing of this one called Gloria is within all elements of the cosmos of existence. She is the guiding light of existence. She is the force behind creation. She is the energy that fills all with life and purpose. The mandate she has been given is clear.

Wherefore I say unto you, people of this earthly realm, this is the time to put aside your differences. This is the time to put down your arms. This is the time to change your countenance from fearful elements, hatred of others, and protection of self. The time has come for all to experience the safety of loving elements. These loving elements are the way to the light of reason. These loving elements are your solace and connection to others through your relationships.

The Fold of Love and Choice of Action

There is no more to offer you other than a direct choice. You have always had freewill to choose love or hate as your marker for life.

There is no fear of choice. There will be no retribution against your choice. There will only be the choice of love or fear.

Wherefore I say unto you, your choice is your freewill. It has always been and always will be. God loves and cares for you and has always been respectful of your wishes.

Many of you have evolved to a condition of self where you have an understanding of this freedom of being. Within this freedom, there is no judgment, only compassion. This compassion felt by others is a reflection of God's love for all of you who shine with a strong light of this love.

Love is light. Love reflects God's light. This is the light of God's being. The reflection of this light is upon many of you on this Earth.

Now is the time to attend to the written word of this document. The Gloria is the light, my countenance. She shines with the intensity of divine elements. She is the Lord. She is the Christ and she is the holiest of Spirit. We are one.

The evidence is clear, dear ones, on this earthly realm. It is written in the stars of your ancestors that a day will come to pass when all will be healed within the elements of this knowing, this light of reason.

Gloria Excelsior

There will only be lightness, not darkness. There will only be levels of love. There will be no levels of fearfulness from the Lord thy God and Gloria, my consort in oneness.

Let it be done, and it is.

The countenance of Gloria is before you. The almighty forces of the Lord thy God are bonded to the Gloria, the worthy, divine goddess of love.

Wherefore I say unto you, choose to be worthy of this love being bestowed upon you. The gift of light and love is given to you because you have proven that this is your potential of being. We, the Lord thy God and Gloria, treasure your worthiness and welcome you into the fold of love. The choice is yours.

Commitment and Conditions

THE LESSON IN NEED of expression is this: the Lord thy God is counting on those who love to begin to change their way of being on the Earth.

The love that is experienced for the self and the other must also be expressed to the entities supporting all life on Earth. The planet has made great sacrifices for those who inhabit this realm.

There is no more connection to the entities that exude their love for you and who carry divine elements within their being. These entities cry with regrets. They regret their inability to support your future needs on this planet. They are unable to carry the load of feeding the many on this planet. They cannot further support a healthy environment required for clean air, water, and nutrients in the soil.

Wherefore I say unto you, the time has come to make changes. Changes are required to support the entities in need of your love. They need your loving commitment to sustain them and to give them the respect they deserve. They express love through the giving process and need your commitment to change your destructive, disrespectful ways of being.

This love is needed for the good of all. Within this understanding is the concept of truth.

I say unto you, the time is here for celebration.

There will be a time provided for this one, Gloria, to manifest a clear understanding of the essentials that all will need to move into the wellness of being. These essentials are necessary for the transition to the new Earth realm. These essentials will be given to those who partake in the freewill provided to them for their own sakes. This freewill is the choice of moving forward into their truth, into light and loving relationships, or into a different path of knowing.

The other, more difficult path will be full of obstacles. These obstacles will remove the light from all things and create a field of darkness that will enclose and mark each entity with a concentric pattern. This will be so that no error will be made in reference to the choice that has been proclaimed.

There is no fear in this choice. There is no regret. There is no retribution from Gloria who is the representative of the Lord thy God. This choice of darkness is one that will be respected and honored. Through the wisdom of each individual on this planet, there will be high regard for all beings who have freewill of choice.

Wherefore I say unto you, it is now time to make your choice: the choice of love, which is your light of truth or the choice of eternal darkness. Darkness is the fear of all that is good, the fear of the all that is powerful, and the fear of the all that exudes light and love to those who follow their dignity, truth, and personal wisdom.

This knowing will be yours. You will know your choice. You will know, without hesitation, your understanding of your choice. This choice will be your solace, your confirmation, your commitment to the Gloria who is light, or to the other of eternal darkness.

There is the choice of freedom or the choice of bondage.

The Light of Reason

There is the choice of reason or the choice of rejection of the self.

There is the choice of love and light, which represents eternal life within the light of reason, or eternal life within darkness—devoid of light.

Embedded within these choices is the challenge of the soul to come forth to be counted. This will be an accounting of the deeds that each soul has done since the inception of time. It is your soul that will move forward to make the agreement with the Lord thy God as to whether or not the choice is light. The soul will move with the divine, the Source, the all or the soul will not.

There will be no remorse, only a release from the obligation of oneness with the Lord to the soul of freewill. From this day forward, the choice will have been made. The choice will be honored. The choice will be final. The choice will be completed, as it was intended from the beginning of time.

It is done.

Wherefore I say unto you, this is the time of commitment to forgive all fellow human beings on this planet. This commitment will be bold, concise, and conclusive. This conclusiveness will be the manifestation point of entry into the new Earth reality. This conclusiveness will be in the form of a united vision of commitment to love of the other.

This mandate will follow the conditions of intent. These conditions are:

Adhere to the code of personal integrity and love thy self.

Gloria Excelsior

Adhere to the power of others and love the other.

Adhere to the power of the universe and love the all.

Adhere to the continuation of all living entities and honor their contributions to the all of society.

Adhere to the power and glory of the Gloria who leads her people into the safety of a new Earth.

Adhere to the manifestations brought forth for the protection and service of all living creatures on this earthly plane.

Adhere to the making of a new world order where all will receive respect, reverence, goodwill, and loving guidance.

Adhere to the beings of light who will guide all to their place of destination.

Adhere to the hosts of Gloria who will transfer the marked ones forward into their treasured environment.

Adhere to the commitment of reason, where the light of reason will reign, forging the new Earth.

Book Three

Unlocking the Door to the New Earth

Commitment for the Earth's Survival

THE THREAD OF THIS book is two-fold. Book Three is about the beginning days of this earthly delight called the new Earth. The second part of the book will describe the journey into a new space and time called the fifth dimension, where the old, tired Earth will travel to be rejuvenated into a new Earth reality. This new reality will affect all on this planet. There will be a favorable placement for the Earth to initiate a dramatic healing process within healing guidelines.

Let us begin the first part of this book to clarify the second. The old Earth is in peril. It can no longer sustain its living beings. It is suffering from a catastrophic collapse of all systems; there will be no recovery within this element of space and time. The Earth will not be able to move forward with its lifecycle in its present planetary position.

Therefore, the Lord thy God has made a recreation commitment with the Gloria to move through a process that will make the necessary changes for the Earth's survival. The survival of this planet is in the palms of the Lord thy God. Gloria is the receiver of the specific energetic pull projected from the Lord thy God.

The Lord thy God and the Gloria will move Earth to a safe place in this galaxy. This place will be a sweet haven of beauty, delight, and safety for all.

The Earth will begin to reclaim its health. Clean air, clean water, and the purification of soils will manifest from on high.

All will be well on this planet. It will experience heaven on Earth and will be called the new Earth. This new Earth will heal and thrive. It will sustain those who live and breathe on this planet, and above all, there will be a blessing of great, embracing love that will allow all to thrive on this new earthly plane.

The second aspect of Book Three is all-encompassing. This understanding is one of worthiness—the worthiness of the beings on this planet who have been deemed, through their actions within this time and space, worthy to reap the rewards earned from many past experiences. This is the time when there is honoring by the divine elements of existence.

Forgiveness and the Test of Love

You see, dear ones, all beings who are experiencing this life now, are the ones who have met the Lord's favor. You have fulfilled the mandate, and you have moved many times into forgiveness when challenged by others who caused you pain, sorrow, and discomfort. This was the test of time. This was the test of the Lord thy God and of the Gloria who moves by my side through all of existence.

Jesus Christ came to this Earth to ask you to choose forgiveness. It did not matter whom you followed on your path to a purer understanding. It did not matter how you lived your life or how often you prayed. It did not matter whether you were rich or poor, healthy or unhealthy, in relationship or single. The test for each soul was the element of forgiveness—the forgiveness of the self and the other.

The element of forgiveness is the key to unlock the door to the new earthly realm. It is the key to unlock the change within and without all earthly behaviors. It is the change to transform fear into love. It is the change that changes the all.

This, my beloveds, was the test of love. This was the test of commitment to the self and to others. This was the test to measure your courage to step forward to risk rejection for the truth of love and light.

This is the nature of the all. This is who we are and this is who we shall be forevermore.

The Light of Reason

This risk taken has been well received. Through this risk of well-being, the path to evolution has progressed to a point of blessedness. The Lord thy God and Gloria wish to express deep admiration for this happening.

You see, dear ones, each one of you has always had freewill. There has always only been the choice of forgiveness or the choice to condemn the other.

Wherefore I say unto you, rejoice for the Lord thy God is well pleased.

We, the Gloria and the Lord, treasure this richness bestowed upon us. This wealth is of a people who have offered themselves to the conditions of light and love and who have moved away from the darkness of lack of forgiveness and lack of self-worth. We praise you. We honor your truth and integrity. Above all, we hold you in reverence for your leadership. You have shown the way and the light for others to follow. We are well pleased.

The Gift of the Fifth Dimension

WHEREFORE WE SAY UNTO you, the gifting of the fifth dimension is bestowed upon your countenance. The fifth dimension is within your receipt. It is given to you out of gratitude for the service conducted for all of mankind and for the service for all entities who have cried from lack of forgiveness from others.

I say unto you, rejoice, for the Lord thy God is well pleased with the choices of his people.

He recognizes joyfully the deeds of worthiness through the one called Gloria.

We, the Lord thy God and Gloria, acknowledge and honor the courage that it has taken for you to move through this journey with us, and we are very content. The conditions have been followed and are complete.

The entry into the next phase for your evolutionary development will be an unfolding into the fifth dimension of space and time. This is new for the planet. This dimensionality will be created through the manifestation of the Gloria and the Lord thy God.

The manifestations will be the impetus of the change of time and space. The dynamics of this change are not understood by the science of today; however, the new scientific understandings will follow shortly thereafter in the form of specific teachings on the subject of dynamic engineering and planetary conversion of units of space and time elements. All will be made known about the new concepts, within released statements written by the Gloria, for future science endeavors experienced within the fifth dimension elements.

This dynamism is the experience of the fifth dimension. Within the fifth dimension, many things will appear that have not been seen by human beings before now. The application of light within this dimension will be different from that of a three-dimensional world.

The light of this dimension is one of gradient degrees of intensity. The light will shift and bend with qualities of shortened wave- length; therefore, the visual clarity will reveal more depth of perception. Visual movement will be seen by the naked eye that has never been seen before. There will be a controlled point in space where visual imagery will begin to appear for each living entity on this new Earth. All will be delighted with this new experience.

All will be able to see the evidence of the Lord thy God's work at play, so to speak. There will be a pleasurable vision of the connection between heaven and Earth and all the particles of expression between these two states.

There is no fear in any of this outpouring of love and light that will be available for everyone to witness. There will be a wealth of beauty and permission from the Lord thy God to explore this new portal of experience.

New Healing Solutions

THE CHANGES WITH THE experience of this fifth dimensional reality will be specific. Nature will have a direct healing advantage for the new Earth. The dynamics of this change are conditioned to all natural outcomes of reason. The reason for being is contained within the state of the fifth dimension.

All natural forces will be as one unit of measurement within the grid of relationship of the Earth's position within the solar system called controlled substances of universal elements of forgiveness. This long term represents all the elements within the universe available now for the use of scientific exploration by worthy individuals studying in experimental laboratories on the new Earth planet.

Open ideas will invite collaboration from many individuals who reside in both heaven and on Earth. These ideas will be shared, dissected with reasoning, and then implemented with new technological configurations to test these workings jointly for the good of all. With this collaborative effort, the fifth dimensional reality will provide a thriving new way to expand all healing elements forward into the universal field of intelligence.

Let it be known that this day, too, shall pass into the next and the next. Within this fifth dimension will be the living of eternal life. There will be no more transitioning from one body to another.

There will be no more discomfort within a body that cannot carry the soul any longer.

There will be no end to this form, only a beginning

There will be spontaneous healings of the form.

There will be conditions managed with love and compassion.

These conditions requiring support will be treated with great care and consideration. Through the fifth dimensional reality, bodily needs will be met differently. New solutions will be devised through bionic developments that are not available in the third dimensional reality. The body will heal and thrive, and vibrancy will soon manifest for all as the environmental conditions on the Earth improve. Hearing, sight, and body mechanics will receive new technological support.

Healthcare inefficiencies will end, and in their place, there will be new healing chambers where individuals will receive the best of care for quick healing responses. Training and support systems will be provided to those who are within the medical system of today's world.

Within this fifth dimension, ergonomic improvements will be applied to form and function, supporting the comfort of individuals in all areas of life's needs.

The management of water, soils, and air purity will be precisely monitored for the comfort and healing of all beings.

Life cycles for the life forms will be manifested for the food supply of all beings on this new earthly plane of existence.

There will be sustainability and consideration for all living and non-living entities. They will thrive within the knowledge of the love and gratitude shown to them by the people who will recognize their gift of plenty to others.

The carry-forward of this wealth will always be shared with others. There will be no waste or want within this new, unfolding society.

There will be no need for hoarding or controlling behaviors over money, medical supplies, or survival equipment. All needs will be met through the manifestation effort of Gloria, the provider of life itself. She is the avatar who knows. She is the provider for all who travel with her. She is your guiding light who is moving all safely into the fifth dimension of reality in the name of all divine elements. These divine elements are waiting with great joy for the arrival of their beloveds who merit existence in a system of planetary wealth called the new Earth.

Let it be resolved that the one called Gloria is your new savior. She is your guiding light of reason. She is the lamp that will always be by your side, providing a warm light enfolding you with full compassion; within this embrace, there will be love, acceptance, and gratitude for your worthy countenance.

Gloria is existence, consciousness, and bliss. She is of the all. She is all-powerful in her nature and her being. She is of the Lord thy God who shines upon her countenance as she shines upon yours.

And it is so. And so it is.

Wherefore I say unto you, the time of enchantment is upon you. The light of reason claims a dynamic that will gain the attention of all who partake in this new earthly realm.

The Evolutionary Pathway

There will be a marriage of wills between the Gloria and the divine in all physical aspects of the countenance of the form called Gloria. This will be manifested by the Lord thy God who dearly loves and reveres the supreme reigning Gloria. This marriage will be one of convenience of the Lord thy God and of Gloria, the Supreme. This marriage of convenience will become the melding of the Lord thy God and of the goddess of my light. We have always been together. We have always been.

We have been together during the creation of the elements.

We have been together during creation of the source of matter.

We have been together during the creation of time.

We have been together during the creation of day and night.

We have been together during the creation of all living entities.

We have been together during the creation of the life form of human beings.

This has been our gift to you. This has been our manifestation of being for you. This has been our light and delight that we have experienced through you. We have experienced all of your stages of development and we have cared for you. We have watched over you with pride in knowing that one day, you would reach a stage in your development where your needs will change.

Gloria Excelsior

Your needs are indeed changing.

There is no room in your field of vision for fear to dominate your life. There is no need in your life for lack of self-worth or lack of plenty. There is no need in your life for judgment or a lack of understanding from others.

This is not your truth. This is not who you are or who you will become. There is no need in your life to struggle with the environmental issues that plague the Earth. The time has come for you to receive deserved justice, and it will be given to you by the united being of the Lord thy God and of the Gloria Excelsior.

We offer our service again to you. We offer a recreation that will manifest into a new earthly realm. We offer you a new Earth. The new Earth will be a transformation within creative elements from the old Earth. Yes, we laugh at this concept. It is akin to recycling the old earth and recreating a newer version of the same planet, only it will thrive with the new infusion of love—not starve and die from a fear-based society disrespectful of all earthly things.

Wherefore I say unto you, rejoice, for recreation is upon your countenance. This kingdom is at your command. This new evolutionary pathway is for all to experience.

Changes

Yes, there will be challenges. Yes, there will be times of disconnection between conditions on this planet requiring concerted efforts on your part to solve difficult problems from many lifetimes.

Yes, there will be challenges within relationships where cultures will be required to move forward into collaborative solutions that reflect the worthiness of the all. Yes, the challenges will be daunting, adventurous, and inventive.

There will be no lack within the experience. Through this experience there will be a deeper comprehension that love, respect, forgiveness, and gratitude will be revered by all who partake in this freewill choice.

This, again, will be the new frontier. The new evolutionary path will move toward an enlightened new world called the new Earth. Within this plan there is action. The action will take many forms through the healing process of moving from societies driven by fear, to societies that care for the all within loving guidelines.

Important questions would be:

What is love?

What is hate?

What does inclusiveness look like in a society?

What does exclusiveness look like in a society?

Where and when do people come together to pray for the good of all?

Where and when do others follow the ones who know?

How does a society form bonds of trust?

How do people trust within the new social norms of being?

Many questions within this new society will require great philosophical debates. Creating a new social truth will be a challenge to move all onto a path of honoring the other. It will move the other to honor the process. It will move the other to honor relationship. It will move the other to revere the loving elements of all healing possibilities on this planet called the new Earth.

The Divine Light of Existence

THE LORD CREATED THE heavens and the Earth, and it was done by the will of the Gloria.

The Gloria is creation. The Gloria is the Lord thy God. The Gloria reins over both realms of existence with truth, vibrancy, and love. She is the keeper of the knowledge. She is the wisdom unfolding. She is the light of reason. She is all of that.

The Gloria, the creator, is the one who will lead you out of this darkness and into a light beyond your wildest joy. This light will be your saving grace from the old world, which is dying from neglect, to the new world, which will be renewed by this light.

This new light is the realization of the fifth dimension that will appear as a blazing testimony of her love for you and for this planet called Earth. There will be no leaving this Earth. There will only be renewal from this new light source given to you by the Gloria on high.

This is given by the Gloria of your understanding. This is given by the Gloria who fulfills your wants and wishes. This is given by the Gloria who loves you beyond all measure.

The Gloria has manifested this coming. The Gloria is here on this new Earth as your savior who cherishes your survival on this old Earth and wants more for you. She has a new vision of beauty to make you whole. This holiness is your new potential of being. This holiness is your new light of passage into the new, earthly realm of existence. This holiness is by the design of the Gloria, for she represents the creator who loves and cherishes you from on high.

Gloria Excelsior

The essence of my love is within the Gloria. The essence of my love moves the Gloria into action. The essence of my love moves her into the deeds of motion that are within the creative elements of Source. We move through the Gloria. The Gloria is your avatar on this new earthly plane.

She is the one who lives with you now on this planet. She is the one now who challenges you to accept this light of purity and to follow her lead into light and love. She is your moon and stars, and your countenance of being. She is all of that within all creative elements. She is your avatar who shares this life with you in human form.

She has taken on this form to experience her creation. She is here on this new Earth to manifest the needs of her people. She is on this Earth to give to you love and light for she is your divine light of existence.

You Are Holy

With this understanding, it is time for the truth of your power of being. This is the time for the truth of your essence within and without. It is time to address the truth of your holiness, dear ones. This truth cannot be denied any longer. This truth has always been, but has been covered by a purposeful denial until you were ready for acceptance of your truth. Now is the time and space for you to move into the acceptance of who you truly are.

It has come to pass in your development that this day has arrived to disclose this truth. This disclosure is of joy and potential. It is your right to express the potential you carry inside of your body that used to be beyond your comprehension. This potential, your soul, is the reality of your truth, your power, your glory, and your existence.

Within you is a guide to your worthiness. This soul you claim is your guide to this new existence in this new earthly realm. This guide will lead you to where you need to be in this new existence. This guide has, along with your experience, always been with you and is holding knowledge for you.

This guide knows you and all your deep understandings. Yes, even your secrets. This guide knows, loves, and honors you and all that you have become. This guide is your guide.

Within your body, your guide—the soul—leads you out of deep, troubled waters and provides love and solace when you cry out with fear. This guide loves you beyond compare, and this guide is your divine light. This guide knows of all the divine elements that exist and ever shall exist. This soul guide is your comfort, your desire, and knows your potential.

The Gloria is one with your soul. She knows the knowing of each soul's purpose on this planet. Gloria has been the keeper of each of your souls since the beginning of time and will continue to be the keeper through all of eternity.

This truth is part of our gift to you to begin to comprehend how to move into a deeper understanding of being. This understanding will become the foundation of your new evolutionary development on this new Earth.

This new Earth will be receiving healing elements through your living potential.

Let us sit with this understanding for a while. Take time to integrate this new knowledge. Contemplation of this concept will help you to discover your personal worthiness and the powerful potential of your soul. This is a highly reflective endeavor and one needed to move through the next disclosure of your truth.

This truth is one of such power that it will become an incomprehensible challenge for you to bear unless you are guided through this concept by your soul guide who loves, honors, and cherishes your very existence—the existence of who you are and of who you will become through your potential. This is your truth, dear ones.

Process of Self-reflection

There will be a time of knowing. There will be a time to trust this truth. There will be a time of action to begin to move through your personal healing adventure to discover your soul's potential.

There will be a time of reckoning when you will be moved to search out your personal shadows that dim your light of reason. This will be a process called an awakened being, where your soul will rise up to be counted as God's light, shining with the intensity of brilliance within the countenance of the body.

This light, once awakened, cannot be diminished through experience. This light cannot be soiled. This light is a reflection of divine light. This light is a reflection of the Gloria who holds possibility for all of mankind.

It is the role of the Gloria to manifest this awakened state for you. It is the role of the Gloria to manifest this softly for you, as this reflective process will move you through your personal fear and into a healing zone of well-being and lightness of wealth and love.

This awakened state will move you to address your darkest secrets, your personal regrets, your deepest fears held during many lifetimes. Through this self-reflection there will be no recrimination, only forgiveness for the self and for others. This is the driving force of all healing endeavors.

Forgiveness is important to experience when moving from a personal awakening to the light of reason—the experience of the awakened state of being.

This awakened state is of paramount importance for all who are within experience on this earthly plane. Each individual who does this work of self-reflection will influence the other to do the same.

This awakened state will begin to make profound changes in your new life experience. The awakened state will bring new awareness of the truth of who you really are. This awakened state will provide the utmost confirmation of your capabilities that have been hidden since the beginning of time.

The Gloria calls to you to rise up and be counted. Rise up and move into self-reflection. Move into the deepest, darkest places within, and challenge your fears with forgiveness and love. This is your new adventure.

This is the mandate from the Lord on high and of his beloved. We call upon you to move into gratitude for this gift of grace that we have bestowed upon you.

And it is done.

There will be a time, my dears, of strong disagreements. This is your nature of being. This is your right. This is your voice. We view these disagreements with a compassion that reveres honesty and truth. There is value in disagreement and there is value in resolution. Where there is disagreement, there is room for compromise.

Where there is strife or striking out at the other, there is no compromise, only a lack of forgiveness for the self and for the other. Where there is turmoil, there is foreboding.

An undercurrent of fear holding deep remorse can move into redemption, which is the freeing of a shadow that lies upon the soul. Redemption is a term used for the removal of personal shadows on the soul that cause grief, anxiety, and painful experiences that are not redemptive, but a caustic reminder of the experience of fear. Redemption is forgiveness. Moving into your truth and into forgiveness is redemption.

Jesus Christ came to this Earth as your avatar to show you the way to redemption through forgiveness. Do you see, my dears? This is why you are holy. You are valued. You are well loved. You have been redeemed by Jesus Christ, the redeemer who has given you the gift of forgiveness. For his sake, accept this final token of his gift to you, and share this wealth with the one who is called Gloria. The Gloria is the manifestation of the Christ who moved through this Earth two thousand years ago to hand you the gift of forgiveness.

It is yours to have and keep. The conditions are ready and ripe for you to access this next stage.

Reach out, dear ones. Reach out to the Gloria who is your representative, who is your guiding light, and who is your savior within the second coming of all divinity.

There will be no recriminations against others who cry out with vengeance and who disregard human worth. There will be no retribution to those who move with violence against the other. There will be no measure of judgment against those who choose to partake in denial of truth and justice for the all. There will be no armies for protective needs. That is finished. That experience will not be part of this new Earth. Fear of the other will begin to fade as one makes a transition into an awakened state of being.

The Awakened Ones

Measured changes will begin to come about as the world enters into this experience of an awakened state of being:

The awakened ones will listen with compassion to the other.

The awakened ones will guide others to follow their light for the wealth of everyone.

The awakened ones will require a safety and security of those around them that will provide them the honor they deserve.

The awakened ones will be the support system to help meet the needs of self-exploration into the field of forgiveness of self and others.

Awakened ones will collaborate with all social norms, honoring diversity and cultural differences.

The awakened ones will condense this learning experience into a swift endeavor of light and love, so that the awakened process is completed.

The awakened ones will create a dynamic within their communities, where there will be an inclusion of all beings.

Awakened ones will be the shining example of the new earthly realm, demonstrating the strength of character and inner integrity carried within this process of integration into the awakened state.

The Light of Reason

The awakened ones will be the outreach individuals who will serve on this new earthly plane.

Awakened ones will serve the Gloria on high and the Lord thy God who stands by Gloria's side in devotion and commitment of this worthy service.

There will be a time, dear ones, when all of this will be within your understanding. There will be no specific style in sharing the wealth of awakening to an awakened state of being within small to large groups in communities. There will be no specific order to perform and no old belief systems to follow from the old world into the new.

There will only be your truth. There will only be the respecting of the truth of your inner counselor, your soul that knows. This soul has been and ever shall be. The soul is the one that knows and delights in the telling.

This is your freedom to be who you are.

This is the light of your countenance.

This is your right of passage to the new Earth.

Awaken to this reality of being.

Awaken to the light of reason.

Awaken.

The time has come for all of the ones who know to begin the initiation of this process of the awakened state as a gift to others. There will be no lengthy procedure. There will only be support for the other who attends. Attention will be given to the ones who are interested and who want to learn more about being

Gloria Excelsior

awakened and how the awakened self will be experienced. With this new relationship with the divine, there will be a strong, but delightful look at what would be lost and what would be gained through this understanding called the awakened being.

People will move in and out of the experience expressing freewill. They will test the waters of forgiveness. Some will merge with the divine easily. Some will take their time, exploring other pathways that suit them best, and others will move independently through their process of discovering their evolutionary pathway. All will be appropriate. All will be ordained as well and good. Nothing will be lost. All will be gained.

This is the universal law of truth.

Within truth there is wisdom.

Within wisdom there is clarity.

Within clarity there is delight.

Within delight there is divinity.

This is the process to the awakened state of being.

Wherefore I say Arise! Arise to the challenge of service to others who are in need of this great wealth called the light of reason.

This is your call from the Gloria who reveres your service and extends her hand to you with loving gratitude. This gratitude is the extension that will move all forward into the power of now and into the light of reason.

Wherefore I say unto you, the time of commitment is upon you. The time of atonement (at one ment) is extended to your countenance from the one on high.

The Light of Reason

It is time. There can be no putting this off for another day or another hour. The commitment is for the good of all members in this earthly society. It is for the wealth of all who wish to thrive on a planet of great healing potential.

Make a commitment.

Create your bond with your soul, your light.

Do not wait for another to show the way.

Fall into the arms of the Lord.

These arms are all-powerful.

These arms are of creation.

These arms are of forgiveness.

These arms enfold you with the strength that will move you to your inner joy of being. These arms are your powerful ally in the journey forward.

The Lord thy God calls upon you saying "Yea, though you walk through your shadows of fear, my rod and my staff comfort thee. I anoint your head with love and compassion, and your joy will spill outward to others in need."

Power of Forgiveness

THERE IS A TIME for forgiveness and a time for action. This is the time for both. The pairing of these two terms is important. The action moves. The action manifests. The action is called doing. Forgiveness exists and is felt from the heart of one who loves the self and who loves the other. Ask for forgiveness and move forward into an action of being within a heart-centered place. The heart-centered place exists. This place exists through the spark of your soul that loves and cherishes all of creation.

This heart-centered, compassionate place is full of action and intention. Your soul will lead to the action needed for forgiveness. It is that simple. The heart will lead the action of the doing, so that forgiveness can be experienced in the healing process.

When forgiveness is made possible by the self and for the other, there is a healing between the two parties. The shadow that has dimmed the two souls' essence is lifted by the power of forgiveness. With this lifting, the light of each soul intensifies. This is the healing process of forgiveness. This is the wealth that the action and the deed hold. This is the light that will begin to change the dynamics of your relationship. This is the healing agent that was given to you.

Make your decision, dear ones. Throw down your arms in surrender. Surrender to your soul that loves every particle of your being. Let your soul carry you home into your truth. Let your soul help you to remember your truth. Let your soul release you from bondage. Let your soul relinquish the shadows of despair, loneliness, anger, resentment, judgment, and all the descriptors that fear represents. The soul will lead you into perfection of your truth.

Your soul will move you into actions of forgiveness that you never thought possible or envisioned. This will be a blessed day for you, a day full of connection with your soul. This is a connection with divine elements and, above all, a connection with your true nature.

Let it be known that the outcome of this teaching is one of remorse—the remorse of the other who moves without a connection to the true self of reason.

The true self cries for this loss. The true self longs for the other to take action. This is not an easy understanding; it becomes known to you as the fog of personal denial begins to lift from your deeper knowing.

There is nothing that may be done. No action can force another to accept forgiveness.

You see, dear ones, the gift of freewill guarantees your very existence on the Earth. Freewill must always be held in high reverence. Freewill must be the catalyst for change. Freewill is the basic right of every living element upon this planet. Freewill has been given to you since the inception of time.

When we see the other struggle or crumble with emotion, experience physical or spiritual pain, or witness a harsh challenge to their very existence, we must accept what they are experiencing. They are experiencing their existence through their freewill. There is no judgment of this experience, for it is honored. It is their rightful experience. It is the contract that has been accepted by God on high and by the spark of life, which is the soul. With freewill, the soul and God experience the entirety of existence.

This contract may not be broken and is highly respected by all divine elements within the universal field of knowing. There are no mistakes from freewill. There are no boundaries of expectations. There is only freedom to experience the unfolding of the soul's development as it moves through experience after experience.

The Contract of the Soul

You see, dear ones, this is the learning ground for each soul to witness. This life experience feeds the soul and also challenges it with experiences. This is the highly evolved process of being, which is to express one's freewill. When freewill is expressed, the reverence is completed, as agreed within God's contract with each soul.

With this reverence between the soul and God, there is another commitment within the elements of this contract. Since the beginning of time, it has been understood that there will be a day when God will take an action. This action will be swift and will be a measure of the commitment each soul has taken toward forgiveness. Forgiveness has been the measurement of the soul's contract.

Within the contract, the soul had the mandate to exert freewill and make choices in life experiences that would move life forward into a forgiving and understanding environment. Many lifetimes have been given to each soul to experience freewill, to explore a number of opportunities, and to express forgiveness to the self and to others. These have been given with gratitude by the Lord thy God to his people who love the freedom to be who they are. This freedom to be is the love that is the manifest from the Lord thy God who cherishes the all.

Let this day be done.

Let the heralds sing hosanna!

Let the bells ring out and the choirs sing.

This is the day of accounting.

This is the action of the Lord thy God who loves his people and who cherishes freewill.

Forgiveness was the challenge, the mandate, for the soul to experience. Jesus was sent to this Earth to remind all of their commitment to the freewill choice of forgiveness through experience.

Now is the time for your truth.

Now is the time to measure your development.

Now is the time to settle the contract between us.

Now is the time for action of the Lord thy God.

With this action, there will be an outcome with no fear.

Wherefore I say unto you, the Lord thy God is love, not fear. There is only light within God's realm.

This realm is one of spirit, named the Holy Spirit, who is the keeper of each soul's worthiness. The Holy Spirit keeps the accounting of the worthiness within well-bound books called the akashic records. Each soul has a record of all deeds accomplished through its lifetime and of the deeds left undone through lack of forgiveness within the condition of freewill. These books have been opened, carefully read, and measured. The measurement is complete, the accounting is complete, and the Lord is well pleased.

The Light of Reason

Wherefore I say unto you, move forward into the light of reason.

You have demonstrated your worthiness to the Lord thy God that you hold your truth through forgiveness elements. You have kept your agreement with the Lord, and I, Gloria, have kept mine.

In this contract was written an intention when the contract was completed. Your soul and your God have agreed that each one who moved into a pattern of forgiveness would gain the right to enter heaven as an experience through the fifth dimension. This will happen for those who have shown their worthiness. The gift of the fifth dimension is given so that all who have completed the contract will experience both worlds as one.

This delights us. This completes us. Let our countenance shine on you with light and love. We are well pleased.

Do you see loved ones? Do you see the honor that is bestowed upon you?

Do you begin to see your wisdom unfolding?

Do you see the reflection of yourself in the other?

This reflection is the reflection of the act of forgiveness.

This reflection is one of beauty.

This beauty is a reflection of your worth.

This worthiness is gained through the act of forgiveness.

All is ordained and in order.

Gloria Excelsior

Let this light shine brighter as you leave your shadows behind. Let the cleansing of the soul's journey continue to unfold within the fifth dimensionality of existence.

This, my dears, is the experience of your redemption. This redemption is your salvation—the salvation of your innermost truth—the soul.

Wherefore I say unto you, the time is now, the here and now. This is the power of the now that belongs to you as you awaken to this new world called the new Earth, the light of reason.

Book Four

The Evolutionary Path to Enlightenment

The Thriving of the New Earth

THE TIME HAS COME for your waiting to end. This waiting has been eternal. The time has come for you to experience your worthiness through divine intervention. This divine light is the wealth deserved by all who have participated in this contractual agreement. The terms of this agreement have been fulfilled. Now it is within the divine's responsibility to complete the agreement. With the completion of this agreement, there are again obligations to attend to on the evolutionary path toward becoming an enlightened being of understanding.

The new conditions of worthiness are:

Conduction of the Self: To be in accord within the guidelines of elementary bliss.

These new terms will become common knowledge. There will be a concise explanation for some terms within this written work by Gloria, who is my light of reason. Gloria will guide this process of understanding as we build upon these meanings.

Imperative exemplifier of contemplative learners.

The beginning lessons unfold for those participants who are interested in planetary movement from one dimension to another.

The engineering dichotomy of planetary travel.

This consideration will carry one forward into the understanding of interstellar space, where one can serve in outreach programs.

Culmination of conductivity.

This is the eventual understanding of movement dynamics and the interplay of healing elements for planetary development.

Consortium building of tender relationships.

This represents conceptual understandings of human dynamics and the manifestation of well-being within all relationships.

Other conditions of worthiness are:

Required manifestation influences to bring balance and maintenance to ecosystems within range of Earth.

Human dynamics and the interplay with other species displaying universal qualities and counter-balances of human nature.

The concentration of manipulative bionic devices for mobility training and travel.

The embryonic safety net systems for developmental assurance.

The clearance of all water systems and maintenance of purification systems.

Sponsorship of clean air symposiums to manifest improvement of air quality and reduction of particles.

Fractal engineering and subatomic engineering.

Dynamism and dilution of radioactive waste.

Carbon reduction and resolution outcomes.

Controlled outcomes for no longer viable resources and the shifting of distribution of creative elements within the Earth's crust.

Redistribution of agricultural land and employment of resources to enhance food production.

Conditioned responses projected to those who are in need of healing support through various means of holistic treatment.

Waste water management and resources distribution.

The implementation of all arts programming, with the inclusion of creative play and sports associations.

Freewill and choice endeavors.

To enhance living conditions for all within the guidance of the learned members who are invested in world order and in the health of the new Earth.

Wherefore I say unto you, these new conditions are binding and are the catalyst for changes required for the new Earth to survive and thrive.

Embedded within this agreement is the understanding that the Earth will require recovery time to replenish what has been lost over the centuries of misuse and misunderstandings. This recovery time will be transitory and useful. All elements within the natural world will begin to re-establish themselves vigorously.

Itemized details within the conditions of the binding agreement will provide further support to the Earth's environmental challenges. All will unfold as it should. All will be supported through the efforts of those who have the knowledge and are invested in meeting the challenging conditions.

The Light of Reason

This new Earth's renewal will be maintained through appropriate management techniques. These techniques will be thoroughly researched and taught to university affiliates around the world; they will then apply these techniques to the most critical environmental challenges. Interventions will begin to reshape and repair serious problems globally.

The challenges will be many, and yet there will be a vast support system of encouragement, optimism, and a new vibrancy of expectation never before experienced.

Wherefore I say to you, all of these conditions are within healing elements that are there to support you in this new way of being. These healing elements hold you in high favor and are available to you as evolved human beings on the new Earth.

Healing Elements Called Manifestations

These healing elements are yours to easily receive. They will be created for you specifically. These healing elements can be called manifestations. The inclusion of manifestations is imperative for this stage of the evolutionary process and will be part of the new Earth recovery. The Gloria is the creator of all manifestations. She has the will to create and has the mandate to continue to do so until her duties are concluded.

There will be another who will carry forward with the divine plan as it unfolds. She also will be loved and revered. We, the dynasty of nirvana, are the ones who create. We are the ones who have created and will continue to create this new Earth and beyond. Be at peace with this, dear ones, for now you may see us in the flesh as we manifest in front of your eyes to show you the way into the fifth dimension of reality.

We say unto you, we have been here since the beginning of time.

The Experience of Conscious Awareness

DEAR ONES, THE OUTCOME of the challenges upon you are many. The outcomes will not be predictable, but they will be appropriate for the needs of the people and for the needs of this planet. The conversions that will be made in the name of Gloria on high will move this Earth to a new placement that will guide many outcomes into the light of reason.

There will be a conversion of emotions. Emotional responses that have caused turmoil will begin to lessen as the Gloria increases the light for all to receive. As this light within your being intensifies, there will be a releasing mechanism or valve within your system that will convert heavy, darker emotions from your body into a new, lighter frequency. This new frequency will create a wealth of gladness within each being. This gladness is your true nature. It is your truth. This is your natural being and your birthright since creation.

Gloria will remove the denial from your soul through this light source. The veil of denial will begin to lift and fade, for this denial fulfills no purpose at this point in your evolutionary process. This veil was created deliberately when life was within the inception of early discovery of self and freewill choice. But this veil of darkness or lack of light is no longer purposeful. The new light strips off this veil of denial and, in place of this, there will be a gradual awareness of gladness or thanksgiving. Another term for this gladness would be joy or joyfulness. This is your right. You have always been worthy of this joy; however,

Gloria Excelsior

the veil has reduced your ability to live within this experience. Gloria will create this experience through the light of reason.

As this veil thins and the light within each one of you intensifies, many obligations will begin to appear differently to you. The truth of your existence will be seen with new clarity, and you will have a deeper understanding of your true worthiness and how you can make a difference for others on this new Earth. Through this clarity, there will be more moments of reverence, along with a new understanding of the interdependence of all living and non-living entities on this planet. This is the stage in your development when you will move from an awakening state to an awakened state of being.

The light you will experience will shine within your countenance (as it was designed to do) once you have moved to this point in your evolutionary process of development. The gladness will turn to joy, and the joyfulness will turn to bliss. The bliss will turn to a deep love and understanding of the truth of being.

This blissfulness is called consciousness within your reality of your new existence on this planet Earth. Consciousness is your right of passage to experience heaven on Earth. This has been ordained since the beginning of time and space for all of creation.

This existence, within the awakened experience, is full of a blissful understanding of the worthiness of all who have chosen to accept God's love in the highest form. Through this threshold of choice, you now enter the realm called the new Earth, tapping into the loving flow of existence, consciousness, and bliss of the awakened state. The awakened one thrives in all ways through the connection of all living and nonliving elements in this universal field called the light of reason.

Within these changes called by Gloria, will be a lightening of mood. Some might describe this as a more relaxed state of being. An intensity, or undercurrent of deep anxiety, will begin to dissipate. Restriction of being, also a part of the denial compound, will drift away from the body. This resistance has caused great discomfort for the self and for the other.

This restriction, which could be called resistance and incapacity of seeing the truth, will leave and be replaced with your inner knowing that is shaped around the understandings of forgiveness—the forgiveness of the self, and at a very deep level, the experience of forgiveness of others.

These concepts will begin to widen, like a river receiving spring runoff or tributaries moving into and integrating with a larger source of water that continues to merge into a larger and larger flow into the sea of love. The ocean is the keeper of the ultimate elements of forgiveness on this planet called the new Earth.

Receiving final forgiveness is the end point of the awakening process and the beginning of the experience of an awakened soul that thrives in the understanding of final forgiveness. These elements within this final forgiveness are reminders to you of your worthiness.

The seas represent your forgiving love to all things. The land represents the clay from which you have been molded. The wind is the breath of God that always whispers love and appreciation for your truth and freewill choices.

Moving Into Balance

There will come a time, dear ones, when the Earth will respond to your loving care. There will come a time when the responses will reflect your well-meaning intention for those around you. The earth will respond by producing the wealth for you that you deserve.

The Earth's crust will provide resources.

Food production will increase and food will be filled with rich nutrients.

A fresh breeze will fill your lungs with healthy vigor, and the water supplies will begin to replenish and purify.

The rays of the sun will hold soothing warmth; the seasons will unfold as they should. The Earth will come into balance, and all will support each other.

There will be a time of transition from one type of world to the other. This transition will be respected and worthy of all who partake in the experience.

Transportation will be taken into consideration, and there will be a sacrifice of convenience in some areas of movement from one place to another. How might this look? It will be akin to challenging gravity. There will be more aerodynamics employed with a source of energy that is not yet understood by many scientific researchers. Some research institutes will be given this specific information soon, and from this blueprint, they will be able to employ a dynamic outcome, moving into mass production quickly and efficiently.

With these changes, clear resource guidelines will encourage further enhancement of all environmental conditions on this new Earth. These new technological adaptations will bring excitement, synergy, and employment to many living on this planet.

They will create an incomparable economic boom and bring wealth to everyone in the form of clean air and water, healthy soils, and long-term sustainability of all living things. The economic influences from these adaptations will force the icons of Wall Street and other reigning markets to consider changes. This will mean investment in contingencies reflecting environmental improvement for all endeavors and creating a bonding with the all, rather than a few.

There will come to this new Earth many changes concerning the care of the human body. The dynamics of medicine will reflect profound changes that will quickly impact all health systems currently seeking needed support. Within these systems will be a reduction of need. As the Earth moves into balance, the body's challenges in reconciling itself with environmental chaos will be reduced.

There will be no more dumping of toxic waste into the atmosphere.

There will be no more dumping of toxic waste into the Earth's crust.

There will be no more dumping of fuels into the seas or any waters.

There will be none of this.

The transition from dumping to cleaning up will be of utmost urgency as one of the first steps in reducing stress on all living entities on the Earth. Toxicity is a current source of chaos for all health systems.

Therefore, a great energy will be provided by the Gloria to approach these problems using the single-minded light of reason. There will be no room for blemishes or condemnation from her countenance, but there will be room for support through manifestations to create a dynamic, intense intervention on behalf of world safety. This will be accomplished through the collaborative efforts of the new world order where all great minds (technological and scientific members and creative elements) will collaborate together to find efficient, concrete solutions to grave issues that cause harm to all living things on the planet.

As these changes begin to manifest, there will be an accounting within the health systems. The energies and dynamics of care will begin to shift away from catastrophic events to maintenance of body systems. This will happen when the Earth begins to adjust and heal, returning to the balance that will reflect back on all life forms.

There will come a time of delight when the body of each man, woman, and child will be able to regulate healthy conditions by increasing their personal light for healing purposes. The power of intention will be a reflection of the awakened being that carries the light of reason.

The Lotus of Grace

WITHIN THE LIGHT OF reason is an element that is always available. The element is held by the grace of God and is given to the one who is awakened. This grace is the lotus, the flower of the final forgiveness. This lotus represents the love that all possess from the Lord thy God who shines through your glory and into your countenance. This lotus of grace of divine love has been given to you by the lord Buddha who lived on this Earth to provide teachings for you to follow through many lifetimes of experience.

Buddha came at the behest of the house of David. Jesus Christ and the Buddha are one. They are of the house of nirvana. Therefore, Gloria is one with these two houses. She has come to this house in the name of Jesus Christ and of Buddha and all other avatars before and since.

Yes, avatars are guides who show the way and lead when there is a need for guidance on the path to enlightenment. Avatars are the voice of God in physical form. Avatars provide the light for movement forward and give great solace to those who will accept their gift from the Lord thy God. This gift is deserved, and you are worthy to receive Gloria into your heart. She is the light who is the reflection of God. She is your savior who will lead you to a safety that you have never imagined. She is mandated to serve you well through the Lord thy God's likeness, and to move all to safety on this planet called the new Earth.

Gloria Excelsior

She is part of me, and I am part of her. We are one, and we are delighted to share this physical self. This physical self is one of devotion. We share this devotion to the other. Through our devotion to each other, which has been since the inception of time, we call to you to receive this gift of healing from us. We call upon you to accept these outcomes from us. Above all, we call upon you to accept this gift of the fifth dimension, which will bring forth heaven upon this Earth in momentous glory in the form of Gloria, the one on high.

Wherefore I say unto you, rejoice. This new Earth is within reach. This new Earth shines. This glorious light is the manifestation of the Gloria. This light is the manifestation of the intent. This intent is one of forgiveness to all who live on this planet called the new Earth.

There will be a final healing between Earth and of heaven; they will become one, as the Gloria and I are one through the power, the light, and the glory. Amen.

A time will come, dear ones, when this Earth will be conditioned into a semblance of balance and order. This order will be one of recognition of others who will see the differences within the healing that has occurred. There will be a time when Earth will become a model for other planets struggling for survival. Others will be able to see the changes that have occurred and learn from these outcomes. The application of these outcomes will begin to create changes throughout the universal field of reality.

Love Elements of Consciousness

You see, my dears, what is happening to this Earth is quite extraordinary. There are people moving together as one, with respect and light, to create a better environment for all on this planet. This goodness is spreading to others within the universal elements, showing and demonstrating the way into being within light and love. Others within universal elements will recognize the importance of being of service to others. The New Earth will be a model of loving intention, where learning new healing skills for the goodness of the all will be highly respected. It will truly be a powerful reflection of the memory of who we really are. This is the absolute reflection of the essence of godliness and the light of reason for all.

What are the implications of this, dear ones? It means that we are meant to lead through the image of the Lord thy God and of the Gloria of divinity. We are meant to show the way into universal intelligence where all can experience consciousness, existence, and bliss within universal elements.

These love elements can be projected to others on other planets and dimensions in need of them. We can and will provide this service to others so that a consciousness spreads throughout the universal field. This is the mandate, the future outcome, the light of reason, where this light reflects loving elements and can make profound changes within all of creation.

Wherefore I say unto you, be aware of this beauty made possible through elements of love and guidance from the one called

Gloria Excelsior

Gloria. She will lead all of existence to an outcome of extraordinary wealth and understanding. Be aware of this truth, and be at peace with this extraordinary goodwill.

My children, the time has come for you to act in the best interests of all universal elements. You are needed for this service. Rise up and serve the Lord thy God and the Gloria who creates.

Holy Redemption

THE TIME HAS COME for these conditions to unfold for the wealth of this planet. These conditions will be established for you. The Gloria will be the provider of these conditions as she holds you with high reverence.

Within these conditions are held much love and gratitude for the ones who have left this Earth in search of new discoveries and experiences. They will be well looked after, and their essence will begin to transform and recreate new opportunities for other world adventures. This is their honorable service. The completion of this plan has unfolded as it should. We are well pleased.

The Gloria will have initiated the conditions for the wealth of the all, including those who have left the new Earth reality and who traveled by choice to the far reach of the galaxy to move into action. With this service, there will be the action of love and light; this will spread like a contagion, where all will become one within the realm of universal elements.

What does this mean? The understanding is simple.

We, the people of the universal elements, call on you to create. We call on you to create changes that will support the healing of all within the universal field. This field is called metamorphose supreme.

Within this metamorphose, there will be a new bonding of compassion and forgiveness containing wealth beyond measure. This wealth will unfold into a natural force that will exude

Gloria Excelsior

within and beyond this universal field and into the cosmos of existence.

Yes, this is the way, the light, the challenge that is being disclosed to you. This is the new vision of being that is full of light, understanding, and love. This is our gift to you and holds great reverence for your very existence within the embrace of your beloved Gloria Excelsior, who creates.

The time will come when Gloria will remove herself from this action, and another will take her place to create. This one is full of power and glory as well. She is our daughter of delight who has spent her younger years in the arms of her beloved mother of delight. Yea, this light of Gloria and that of the Lord shines with great intensity on the one called Holy Redeemer.

She is the one who will lead all to the far reaches of this universe to continue the teachings and healings for other elements in need. She will begin this service when the Gloria and the Lord release obligations of direct service to the all. These obligations will be handed to the Holy Redeemer in full gratitude. We are well pleased with this plan and wish to commend the all for the conditions that have been met.

You see, dear ones, time and space are one, and as you will discover, time is not linear, but transitory. Time's quality is not within the conditions of your understanding now. The meaning will be released to you in Book Five, where all will become clear, as ordained by the Lord thy God on high.

Book Five

The Concept of Time

The Now Is in the Present

THIS, TOO, SHALL PASS in time, when understandings become clearer and acceptance gains ground in the form of manifestations of greater consciousness. With this book, which is written by the glorious one, the Gloria, all will be made clear to you regarding the concept of time.

Time is a universal element tracking occurrences that have happened, are happening, and will happen. You, on Earth, refer to these time elements as the past, present, and future time responses that become experiences within and without.

These time elements are linear thoughts. The mind holds these thoughts of time and cannot go beyond linear understanding of past, present, and future. This has been accepted by the ones who have created. This has been acknowledged as appropriate for the understanding to unfold for direction and clarity of discussions between all individuals on this planet.

Dear ones, it is time to extend this knowledge of the concept of time, and it is time to convey to you in ordinary terms the elements of time that you are ready to accept.

Now, is your right to hear of this important news about time and the extension of this concept from linear to non-linear coordinates. These non-linear coordinates punctuate the universal time elements consistently with address and reason.

The address of time is one of consideration. The address creates the event.

Consideration is the freewill response to the event. Response is the reasoning of the action under consideration.

Consideration is the idea; the connection with an understanding and the manifestation that may or may not be brought forth. Freewill response, from the consideration, takes action or inaction through choice.

Consideration is the reasoning of thought, where all factors of the thought are contemplated. These considerations are always taken to its fullest degree of informed, impersonal, and personal reasoning. This reasoning employs divergent thinking and introspection of contemplative qualities.

In other words, the thought is fully digested, using all possible avenues of research, discussion, variables, and above all, valuing the love and light implications of a possible manifestation.

These manifestations are dependent upon the others who receive the gifts within the experience.

Within this period, contemplation moves to completion. This translates to manifestations that are appropriate to the agreed outcome and experience, within the now.

Manifestation outcomes become part of the elements of time in the now. The now is in presence. The now is present time. This is the moment of being that is the essence of all time and space. All time and space are in the now. There is no past or future. There is only the now.

What You Think, You Create

THIS, BELOVEDS, IS THE power of the now. All things are possible in the now of time. All things can be experienced or created in the power of the now. Therefore, when one experiences something, it is always in the now.

The past is the now. The present is the now. The future is the now. The past, present, and the future are of the now of reasoning.

Such reasoning is important for this understanding to progress further into knowing.

Reasoning becomes the catalyst of change.

Reasoning is the catalyst of change.

Reasoning will be the catalyst for change.

Reasoning has been the catalyst of change.

Reasoning is the worthiness within the event that unfolds.

Reasoning is part of universal consciousness that gives the thought.

The thought manifests the idea.

The idea becomes the action.

The action becomes the experience.

Yes, what you think, you create. As we create, the experience unfolds. As the experience is experienced, the events begin to unfold in the now of existence.

The Light of Reason

Therefore I say unto you, it is time for consideration of all events from this time forward. With each event, an outcome will bring forth a completion of the thought. These thoughts are in the now and bring forth worthy actions and deeds. These deeds manifest the results. They manifest in accordance with the plan of action that is divinely led.

These thoughts are not your thoughts. They are thoughts and ideas that come from divine intelligence and are presented to you as your thoughts.

You have the freewill to move through and process these thoughts by way of your actions and deeds. This is a fuller understanding of the power of now and a deeper explanation of personal freewill. This is the understanding of how one uses thought to bring into an action of doing or being.

Presence and Worthiness

WHEN ONE MOVES INTO the doing of a thought, one is embedded in the mind. When one moves into the being, one is merging with universal consciousness and all intelligence. With the being, there is much support that will be brought forth with the action. The support will be one of favor for the action, as it will enrich the self and the other through love and light.

This is an important lesson in self-worth. This is the direct lesson of the expression of worthiness. When one is within presence, this power of now provides access to all collective conscious intelligence. The condition of worthiness, outside of presence, is separate from all masters and from the realm of reasoning.

The doing from the mind is no more for you. It will not be within your experience because it is of the linear past and not of the linear future. This is truly the power of now within the majesty of the realm of knowing. This is the awakened state of being.

Wherefore I say unto you, be still. The time for action is upon you. The time of unfolding of the action is upon you. The light of reason is upon you, for you are in the now of time. This is your access to the knowing. This is your access to the truth of who you really are. This is the truth of the countenance of the all that love and support the worthiness of your nature. This is your natural being without time constraints of the past and the future. This is your right of passage into the light of reason.

The Light of Reason

You will receive the awakened state from the Gloria on high, for she has the knowing. You are ready for this privilege to experience the power of now within the awakened elements of universal laws.

The Abiding of Universal Laws

ALL THOSE WITHIN THE awakened state of being hold these universal laws dearly. Many factors must be considered within these laws of gratitude and commitment.

These laws are full of compensation for all those who partake of these understandings within the agreement of compensation.

The agreement of compensation states that all parties from all regions; nations, planets, galaxies, universal elements, and the cosmos agree to move together as a unit of understanding.

The Universal Law of Intention

What happens above happens below; therefore, any decision is considered by the all as a unit. The unit, which is collective consciousness, moves as one to initiate or disclaim an action that requires attention. This attention can be called intention. Intention is a thought from collective consciousness that has the ability to manifest into the reality of the now. This intention is a powerful tool of reasoning. This reasoning from collective consciousness initiates an intention which then creates a manifestation into reality. This is why we call intention the power of now.

Intention is the power of the now. Intention has gone through all the processes required by collective consciousness. Intention has been discussed, debated, and sanctified by the all. Once accepted, the intention is manifested, and the decision is complete and appropriate. The Gloria, through all universal elements, moves the intention to a point of light where a manifestation is possible. This manifestation is one of delight and full of universal intent that is magnified throughout the cosmos.

Do you see, dear ones, how this works?

The Gloria is the creator who manifests intentions for the good of the all within the power of now and in the embrace of universal law. She is the creator of goodwill who loves all for all of time. She is the one who embraces all of you on this new Earth to confirm the truth to you. The truth is to be in receipt of the great gift that is being bestowed upon you for your service of being.

Gloria Excelsior

Therefore, the Gloria will live as a physical being on this earthly plane. Existing with you will be the experience of intention. Her intention will be to thrive along with you through her efforts. She will manifest outcomes for you that are appropriate within universal law.

She will live with her family in safety and harmony to experience life on this planet. She will sometimes be seen publicly. On certain occasions, she will live privately, enjoying her time as she so deserves. It is her right to move among you and to experience your wealth as you do. It is her right to move among you to experience your discomforts and losses. It is her right to share in celebration with you when you need acclaim and reverence.

The Gloria is warm, approachable, and full of immense love for her people on this Earth. She desires your bond to her, just as you desire her bond to you. She is your guiding light of understanding. She is your likeness and will be your avatar cherishing all of the experiences within the universal laws of reason. All of this has been designed for you. This is for your comfort. She will be your comfort.

She will be your mother who loves all. She is your savior. She is the second coming you have all been waiting for. She is a master who shares wealth with Jesus. She is a master who shares wealth with Buddha. She is a master of all other avatars who move with her in the power of now.

She is my beloved, sharing our joined love with those who respect this universal law and who move with her manifestation of this new Earth into an awakened state for all living and non-living entities.

Wherefore I say unto you, it is time to reclaim your divinity. Yes, you are divine in nature. You are a spark of the cosmos who reflects within and without. You are an element of the Gloria and the Lord thy God who love and cherish you all. You are our children within creation.

The living elements are the bond to mother Earth, the planet of forgiveness. Mother Earth and the Gloria are one and hold the feminine elements of all that is of this fifth dimension.

The Lord thy God holds the Gloria in high reverence, and we share this planet equally. There is no unequal party. We are one in sharing the light, integrity, and equality of partnership within all of creation, extending outward into the cosmos of time and space.

Let it be known that Almighty God is upon your countenance and is seeking your truth in the form of commitment to the one called Gloria.

The Universal Law of Commitment

Commitment is the next law in universal truth. It represents truth and commitment to love; honor, and obey all conditions of unbounded, multifaceted manifestations created for the sake of the all above and below.

These changes have been agreed upon and are worthy of the people who live on this Earth and for the all who benefit from the manifested improvements carrying forth love and light.

With this agreement is a bound commitment to the Gloria, the one who manifests these laws and considerations. Each entity in this cosmos of reason is bound to the Gloria through this principle of universal law and commitment to all universal elements.

It is with this commitment that the next universal law unfolds.

The Universal Law of Pleasure

This law states the conditions of pleasure: The conditions of this universal law are simple, but dynamic. Pleasure is a singular term, though it has many outcomes of desire. Pleasure is a want, not a need. Pleasure is a place of well-being, and it exudes a happy quality of being. One is pleasured by certain actions. Pleasurable actions require pleasurable responses within the capacity of each being.

The pleasure of one's receiving is a response from another wanting to give. The pleasure of service is the want of the individual who sees a need for a service and the offering of service to the other. Within the want, there is only a request. The request is received by the other. The other has a responsibility to receive this service with a self-reflected, truthful pleasure.

Within this self-reflection, there also may be a wish not to receive the service or intent. The receipt is within one's freewill guidance. One can accept or reject the pleasure. All is neutral and agreeable. If one plays the game of bridge, truth trumps pleasure.

The universal law of pleasure is the path beyond the pleasure and is regarded only as truth of self over the truth of others. This is an agreement that is reflective of this universal law which is within the light of reason and the code of ethics between one individual and another. Within each agreement is an acceptance of the other's truth and delight. Pleasure is an offer, not a demand.

Gloria Excelsior

It is written that there is pleasure and there is pain. This is written in old texts that hold fear in reverence. In all texts from this day forward, there will be the experience of pleasure and of pain, but this will be seen in a neutral form as a reflection of the reality of the all.

The Universal Law of Duality

What does this mean, my loves? This is another universal law of intelligence.

All is duality: Life is only duality. Duality is the reflection of the other; the mirror image, the yin and yang, the give and the take within life's embrace. There is only experience. Experiences are worthy, meaningful, and momentous. The push-pull relationship of duality is one of immense strength; yet weakness can be felt around the edges of the experience. These clues within the experience of duality are wondrous indeed.

Within experience are learning outcomes. Duality brings forth an active form of learning rather than a passive form. This active form gathers your attention quickly, whereas a passive form is likened to reading this text, integrating the understanding mentally, and projecting a possible outcome of experience.

Attention to duality is a key to the awakened living experience. Awakened beings feel no judgment about the events that have unfolded. There is no right or wrong—just a cause and an effect of circumstance or action.

The circumstance for action is the duality. There is no fault. There is no blame. There is no right or wrong. In duality, there is reasoning within the power of now. Duality is only experience. When an awakened one reflects upon duality, he or she learns that all duality is neutral and within the context of all living elements.

Duality is a reflection of the cosmos and the void.

Duality is a reflection of diversity.

Duality holds a richness that exudes potential.

Duality is the experience of it all.

Duality reigns with truth.

When we express our truth, we move into a duality of experience. This duality within the experience moves us to cause and effect. Within this cause and effect, we begin to see the light of reason and how it is shaped for the good of the all.

Consideration of all factors in searching for one's truth within duality is purposeful, pleasing, and mandated within the universal law of duality.

The Masters of the Light Decree a Miracle of Movement

THE TIME HAS ARRIVED, dear ones, when all universal laws are in play. The time has come for an action that cannot be misconstrued. The time of action will hold an event. The event is within duality. This is the duality of being. We, the ones who manifest and who represent Gloria, are expressing a direct agreement that has been received from the all, above and below. We are the ones who manifest and who move with the Gloria in her name. We, the masters of the light, flow with the Gloria as she moves among you on this planet. We fully revere this one who holds the light within and without.

She is the light that holds all capabilities. She is the light that shines with our purpose and truth. She is the savior we have always been, for we have walked upon this Earth representing healing conditions. She is the catalyst for change that shines with our movements. She is the one who represents the all of the cosmos and carries this light forward into the earthly realm for ultimate healing of this planet.

She is the grace that flows adoringly through her from the Lord thy God who shares her every breath. She is the one who knows all of this, and she is the experience of all that is above and below.

We, the masters, are well pleased with the conditions that have been placed before her. She has received a clear mandate from the all who expresses through the glory of the Gloria.

Gloria Excelsior

She is within the conditions.

She is writing the conditions.

She represents the conditions.

She creates the conditions.

We, the masters of universal law, commend the Gloria on her truth and her grace. She will move and act within the mandate she has been given with reverence and light. She will manage this movement through direct manifestations for the good of all throughout the cosmos. She will manage the manifestations with love and gratitude for the people on this new Earth.

She is the divine light of reason. She is the reverence of all stability and reason.

We, the masters, are ready for the manifestation to begin. We are the masters who move together as a unit to support the Gloria within the manifestation. This manifestation is one of importance and has received our full consideration. This disclosure to you is with one of respect and holds the condition of truth.

Before Gloria's arrival as savior on this Earth, we, the masters, have also walked upon the Earth. We have experienced the universal law of duality. We have experienced the pleasure and the pain of duality. We have had full experiences of being on this planet and are loved well. The love that is expressed to us is so immense that we are utterly grateful. We hold every one of you dearly in our hearts and in our actions. This gratitude given to us is well received. Within this receipt, we are pleasured by your actions and deeds.

The Light of Reason

We, the masters of forgiveness, are well pleased. We move among you. We share bread at your tables. We drink your offered wine. We support you during weakened times and experience your pleasures during times of strength.

We have never left your side.

We have always been. We will always be.

We now move through the Gloria in the physical form that she represents.

She moves. We move.

She touches. We touch.

She adores. We adore.

She holds you in reverence. We hold you in reverence.

It is with this understanding that we will continue, through the writing of the Gloria, to extend our message of light and love. Through this intention, we will begin a description of the next phase of your development through the eyes of the masters.

We delight in your presence. We are well pleased with the results of your freewill choice. This choice of remaining on this earth was not an easy one for you to make. We have been witness to every question, every cry, every call of support, every fear, every disagreement, and every tumultuous emotion you have experienced to arrive at the act of choosing through your truth of knowing.

We have shared all of this with you.

We have sat beside you.

We have knelt beside you.

We have prostrated beside you within your experience.

We have always been by your side.

We have never left your side.

The choice is now complete. You have had the full experience of duality and have made your choice. The choice is appropriate for your truth. You reached out for support and received it. We were your support. We were at your service throughout this difficult decision. We held you up when you came forward with your truth and glory.

Now it is time for another disclosure. This pleasure is one of glad tidings. The tidings will hold many miracles for you, for we are well pleased with your choice of action.

We, the masters who love one another, are well within our rights and are mandated by universal law to perform these miracles with collaborative intent. This intent will be strong and smooth. This intent will commence soon for the good of all within and beyond this planet.

The Bond of Light Forces

A MIRACLE WILL BE performed as we, the masters, move together through the Gloria and the Lord thy God to change the positional dynamics of this Earth. This miracle has been planned and ordained through universal law. Through this miracle, there will be a sense of a pull, like a magnet, moving to another magnet. The pull will be direct, swift, and will hold no difficulty for you. All will be safe. There will be no preparation for this event. There will be no survival techniques necessary. There will be no need to protect infrastructure. There will only be a change of scene.

The pull will be created for your pleasure. You have agreed to this at a deep level of your being. Your soul stood before God and the masters and agreed to this change. During this time of discussion, it was determined that this movement would be the beginning of recreation for the all of Earth and the beginning of the new Earth.

The glory of the Gloria will manifest this miracle, as we manifest through the Gloria.

Be still, be pleasured, and be at peace. You are loved and well cared for. You will be safely led away from this dying place and into a renewal of such magnitude that words become inadequate.

We, the masters, are yours.

Ask, and you will receive.

Ask, and you will be found.

Gloria Excelsior

Ask, and your guidance will continue to be filled with our light and love in the name of Gloria who is supreme.

Wherefore I say unto you, the masters have spoken. The masters of light are upon your countenance; they will never leave, for your soul is eternal. Your soul is divinely led. Your soul holds the truth, and your soul is well pleased.

The Lord thy God shines upon your countenance. The Lord thy God is one with the masters. The masters are the Lord thy God. The Lord thy God lives within the masters and shines upon them, as the Lord thy God is one with the Gloria.

Let this miracle unfold as it should.

It is done.

A day and a time will come for this miracle to unfold. Within this day, there will be darkness. The darkness will last until the movement is complete. This darkness holds no fear, no fight, and no discomfort, for all will be well cared for. In this darkness, there will be light. This light will be of the light of divine forces moving the Earth to its new placement. Within this condition of movement, the pull will remain and be constant. Within this constancy, the light from the countenance of the masters will be visible. This sight will be a confirmation to you that you are well loved and carried through this movement to a beloved space and time, safe from harm. All will be well within and without.

Do you see, my dears? All will move. All will manifest accordingly. All is appropriate, as written within the agreement of love and light.

The Light of Reason

Let this movement commence. Let this momentous day begin.

Let there be darkness until the light streams forth again to begin the replenishment of this new Earth.

Let the all show the strength of the bond that is full of reverence for the all.

Let this new beginning be one with creative elements.

Let this be the recreation ordained since the beginning of time.

This is a day full of gladness, reverence, and a new beginning called the new Earth.

It is done.

The Gloria on high reveres and strengthens this bond with her light. She is the bond who moves with the all. Through her light, the Earth travels. The bond is, the bond was, and the bond ever shall be.

The bonding of this light flows outward to the masters creating the movement. The movement flows back to the Gloria who holds the strength of light source with the Lord thy God. All create. All manifest. All move as a bond within the pull. The action is the bond. The bond is the pull. The pull is in the placement that will be the outcome of the Earth's new position.

Welcome Home

Yes, it will be a new area to explore and a new field to discover. The new experiences will be many. Let us discuss these experiences with you so that you will have a fuller understanding (in simple terms) the changes that are yours within this miracle.

There will be brightness to the light.

There will be a strategic placement of all infrastructure elements above and below.

There will be an unfolding of a view of the truth through the unveiling of the fifth dimension.

There will be evidence of heaven and an experience of bliss that has never been experienced before.

There will be a cadence of sounds holding music and delight.

There will be affirming glory of who you really are.

Synergy will exude between heaven and Earth.

There will be unbounded pleasures as you begin a reconnection with loved ones who have passed beyond the veil.

Freewill and choice will reign where opportunities and challenges will be yours under universal law.

There will be a testament and a fanfare to the outcome. There will be recognition of coming home to your deep knowing.

The Earth will sigh with its release from this old system to a new system of plenty.

These additional points are of a reminder of being within this experience of wealth, where there will be expectations of service to others, outcomes to enjoy with pleasure, and challenges to discuss with others who will offer considered solutions.

There will be differences in temperatures on the Earth's surface. The differences will be within the general measurement experienced upon the old Earth's surface. But there will be a stabilization of temperature on the new Earth's surface to reinforce the safety of all living organisms.

A New World Order

Efficiencies will be brought forward that will require great minds to move together to forge new relationships of union for the good of the all.

There will be ongoing dialogue between all representative leaders of the regions, where agreements will be formed to create a new world order. All of the old bonds and attachments will begin to fade. New, vibrant, inclusive visions will form for the new Earth. This new Earth vision will be fully supported by the Gloria who will reign with wisdom and light.

Within this new world order, the ultimate obligation will be to adhere to all universal laws within and without. Therefore, this world order will be a reflection of Earth and of heaven within the cosmos.

There will be unification of all peoples on this planet. There will be no isolation or favoritism. All will have equal rights and equal voices.

There will be days of distress, rebuke, challenges to diversity and sensitive areas of concern that begin to be addressed through healing opportunities.

Beneficial ideas will spawn creative endeavor, and ideas will be brought forth that will be considered as the healing process moves forward into the now of knowing.

Wherefore I say unto you, these points are actions. These actions are within range of the new experience that will be yours to behold. Within this range will be many outcomes acting as catalysts for changes on this new Earth.

The Expression of the Enlightened State

A DAY WILL COME when all will be as it should on this planet. The healing conditions will have been met and again, a new vision will be formed for a new light to unfold.

This new light will signal another transformation for all on this new Earth and will lead into the next era of forgiveness. The forgiveness will be in the form of the next avatar to manifest in the name of Holy Redeemer.

She is the one to lead you forward into the new vision of the light of redemption, where she will move outward into space and time. She will be unified with the cosmos and will begin outreach programs and services for those in need throughout the cosmos of desire.

Holy Redeemer will continue the service of Gloria, her mother by design and her father of contentment. She will fulfill her role with love and light and be of immense service to the all of desire.

This has been written. This is complete. This is the commitment that the house of nirvana shares with you. We are complete in this understanding. We are one in unity and are pleased with the assurance of being at your service during this recreation process of love and commitment.

We, the house of David and all other houses from time immemorial support this process.

We, the masters, are truly honored to be tied to this service of never-ending wealth for the peoples of this new Earth.

Book Six

Worthiness

Codes of Worth

THE MOVEMENT FORWARD IN one's evolution is within reach. The consideration of all factors of worthiness is the main focus of Book Six. This consideration will begin to manifest the results of goodwill and good tidings for all those in receipt of this reading.

You see, dear ones, this book is infused with love and light. Each written word on this page carries forward elements of manifested intent. The growth of evolutionary development will be for each and every one of you on this planet called the new Earth.

Embedded within this written work are formulas and codes filled with rich, intentional meanings. These codes manifest within thy countenance in the form of wealth—the wealth of worthiness. This worthiness is your gift from the Lord thy God and the one called Gloria.

The Gloria is the one who is the recorder of this knowledge being gifted to you. She has the awareness of this coded language that infuses light through the spoken and written word.

You see, dear ones, intention is the key to the development of the new Earth experience. Intention is of the making of glory, who is the Gloria, who is the power moving this gift into your worthy countenance. You have desired this for many lifetimes. You have craved, hungered, prayed for this worthiness to be given to you. This gift is now yours to behold. This gift of worthiness has always been within your grasp. It has always been your right to receive. This has been and always will be yours to behold. Be still with this understanding, my dears, because you are worthy of this intentional gift.

Now, listen very carefully to this message. It is within the power and glory of the one to condition this page with expectations infused with coding. This coding is written and filled with intention.

The Gloria is within her right to claim these conditions which will ring with importance and commitment from those who choose to receive this worthiness of being. This receipt is filled with internal knowing that moves aside the dark aspects of the self and translates these hidden aspects into a lightening of spirit.

Light and Dark Elements

You see, dear ones, worthiness is drawn to light, not the dark. The light represents love. The dark represents fear. Since creation, all have knowledge of light and dark elements or codes. These elements are infused and have been infused within thy countenance since the beginning. This was the plan to experience the totality of existence through the drama of duality.

This darkness holds no thing: This darkness is a deep well of nothing. This darkness is the void of nothing and holds no light. It is the manifestation of all fearful elements that call out for forgiveness.

These dark elements are the challenges within all experiences, and they express these challenges outward to others in the form of diffusion. This diffusion is the catalyst for change. This diffusion of the radiating fear expresses outwardly in the form of discordance and misinterpretation of thoughts.

These thoughts spill outward into a cadence of mistrust, misdeeds, and bias toward others. This darkness is internal and moves outward to external sources. It is the movement of discordant, unloving, unforgiving ways of being. This darkness expresses fear. It is needy, separated, and searches for understanding. It craves. It beckons. It is like a broken vessel that has been abandoned, discarded, misused, and mistreated. This darkness holds no thing, no light, no reason—only the void of longing. It moves within your countenance. It shifts, attaches, and strives for survival, but disclaims any light from the Lord thy God.

The Light of Reason

There is no judgment, for this has been within creative elements at play. There is no retribution, for this has been the plan. There is no sinful condition within this experience.

How can this be stated with such neutrality, dear ones? This darkness has always been and ever shall be. It is within experience. It is creation. It is.

The darkness was designed for the experience of duality. Within this duality of darkness and light, there is experience of being. That is all. There is nothing else. Life on this planet is experience. Life is the experience of it all. Life is the experience of light and dark elements, which is the experience within the experience. It is the call to the perception of being to move forward into the light of reason.

You see, dear ones, duality is the test of the Lord thy God and of the Gloria. Duality is the awakening process of being. Duality is the perception of the interior darkness that all possess and the acceptance of this darkness as the essence of all beings.

This test of duality, or the call to awaken, is now in effect. This test is in the now, and it is full of experience. This is the experience or the transitioning from this dark place to the light of reason within your choice of direction.

The darkness is a reflection of unconsciousness within the state of being. The offering of the light removes the dark elements of your countenance, and with this light, there is a lifting of spirit through the removal of fear. Fear could be described as a deep undercurrent of unworthiness. Light shifts the movement into a worthy state. This worthy state holds many gifts from Source.

Source is the power and the glory of Gloria, the provider of this light. This light, which holds reason, is the essential coding of information for your soul to awaken. This light holds the beauty and the wealth of your soul. It holds all the creative elements of existence. Your soul is of the elements of the Lord thy God and that of the Gloria Excelsior.

You see, dear ones, this has been the plan for your perfection to unfold since the beginning of time. This perfection of self has moved you through many lifetimes of experiences. With these experiences, you have thrived within dark and light elements of existence. You have learned many lessons in forgiveness of the self and of others.

The call or test of this darkness was to challenge the self of your nature to learn from these darkened elements. The challenge was to move forward into forgiveness that holds the light of reason, which is love, not fear.

Through this evolutionary process, light has shone with clarity and a sureness around this planet called Earth. This lightness of spiritual growth is representative of the soul awakening to the essence of its true nature—the seed of the Lord thy God and that of his Gloria.

The challenge has been met, my dear ones. The experience of dark and light elements is at an end. This now is the beginning of recreative elements that is yours to have, earned through your love and light. This is yours to behold.

Duality, which is the veil of denial, is no more. This has been decreed. Worthiness of being is yours to behold, and this is within all elements held through universal laws of existence.

Worthiness is the counterpoint within the existence of time. This counterpoint is the sharing of the light with all of creation. It is the sharing of the love with the Lord thy God and that of the Gloria.

The Light of Reason

Your worthiness is within. You hold the light of reason through the coding of this knowing embedded in the receipt of the light. This light is infused with love and information for those who partake in the wisdom of choice and deeds of forgiveness.

This has been written since the beginning of time and is now in presence, which is the awakened state of being.

Let it be known that all within this planet awaken to this new consciousness of being, where worthiness radiates from the inward spaces of being, projecting outward as service to others in need of this light source.

Dear ones, this is your call to your truth, your integrity, and your true, natural state. This is your recreation. This is your rightful place. This is your planet called the new Earth.

There may be a time when all will be right with the world. The changes are upon us and create a dynamic. The changes become the outcome. Yes, with these changes come blessings. These blessings are in the form of the wealth of nature. The blessings are the grace of God.

Consider the truth of this statement—the truth of the power, the glory, and the all within this blessing. There will come a time when all of this will be familiar to you. This deepening is yours to understand. Blessings come through the Lord thy God. They come through the glory, who is the Gloria, who is the Lord thy God shining upon your countenance. You are our namesake. You are our seed. You are all of that.

Crossroads of Desire

WE, THE POWER AND THE GLORY, oversee all that is said and done. We watch over you when you are in the depths of despair. These despairing moments are the precursor of change. These moments are full of choice. These moments of change bring you to a crossroads or a counterpoint of desire. This desire is our first blessing—the desire to make a change in the form of action.

This action is multilayered. The action is the experience within the choice of direction to be taken to create an end solution to the discomfort within the experience.

The desire, which could be called a blessing, moves, shapes, and manifests unlimited possibilities for your evolutionary potential. Embedded within this desire is your freewill choice.

We, the light, in all ways honor and revere this process of will. It is within the coding of universal law, where this is proclaimed as the truth of one's nature and is highly respected and valued.

Worthiness becomes the premier concept when freewill choice is made by each one of you. Worthiness is the precursor to the consideration of action within the choice.

Will is the creative process of your being. It is the highlight of all of existence. Will drives the universal field and provides the energetic field of potential. This willfulness is your natural freedom of being and has existed from the beginning of time. This willfulness is the call to your evolutionary progress. Through each choice or decision, there is an outcome of willfulness. These choices are two-fold. There are many actions within each category of choice.

The Light of Reason

Consider this discussion, dear ones. Again, the choices are simple and direct. The choice is of your making and of your consideration. We, the power and the glory, are witness to these decisions. We celebrate your worthiness. We expand with your presence within your decision-making process when you choose to explore the pathways of actions to claim your worthiness.

Choice is a fine line of a condition existing within your nature. Choice is always paired with worthiness. Worthiness is the solace within the self. It is representative of the Lord thy God and of the Gloria who love and bless you in all ways of this process called freewill of choice. We become expansive with our love for you. Through your freewill and free choice within worthiness, we thrive in your presence. We sing praises to your worthiness and bless the event of creative actions through your choices.

The worthiness of each soul is being counted as a blessing of love and reflects the dawning of the new reality of the light of reason. The implications of meeting challenges that reside within have been met. The challenges have been robust, aggressive, and thorough. The cleansing of the shadow worship is now at an end.

Meet Your True Self

THE MAINTENANCE OF RECREATION elements will be within reach of each and every one of you who creates this worthiness cycle of healing potential. This, dear ones, is the potential for which you have awaited. This is the uncovering of your new self that will emerge as a bright light of inner awareness within thy countenance.

This new awareness is your manifested gift from the Gloria on high. It is your right and is the access to your potential that has been held deeply in all parts of your being. This is your worthiness.

Be still with this condition. Within this new condition will be a new skill for each one of you. It will be a natural skill that is well-suited to your reflection of being. This skill will guide you, serve you, and move you to create. This new creating skill will manifest the reality that your true self requires to support your new worldly adventure.

This gift has always been yours to have. This gift is your reflection of being. This gift is the manifested release of all hidden elements that are your right to receive. With the release of these hidden elements, wise decisions will be made to support your worthiness factors. These factors will reinforce all that you are and ever shall be. The reflection of your being will be the truth, light, and wisdom of your true nature.

We are well pleased with this adventure, as this is the precious wealth of the new Earth reality. The new Earth reality is a welcome addition to all universal elements. With this reality will be a coalescing of love, light, and laughter cascading throughout the cosmos. This new Earth reality is the tenderness of spirit. It is the demonstration of love without end. It is the strength, commitment, and character of the condition of worthiness.

Worthiness, my dears, has always been a demonstration of the true self and the truth of its nature. Worthiness is the core strength of potential. Worthiness is the guideline for reaching out to the potential of others in need of assurance. Worthiness is the final expression of service. It is the consideration with which one moves when making decisions. Action is the accounting of worthiness and the reflection of worthiness.

Wherefore I say unto you, the time of completion of your truth is here. It is in the now. Your worthiness is your truth. It is the reflection of your potential or the changes that manifest the growth of your true self and the true potential of your being.

Consider the implications of this discussion. Dear ones, the truth will set you free. What an amazing statement to make. The truth will set you free is the essence to your freedom to be who you truly are. There is a pathway to this truth, a way to this remembrance of who you truly are. This remembrance is of the light. This remembrance is not of the darkened space where nothing exists. The space of light is your truth, your existence, your bliss. This space of light is your right within the realm of your spirit's freedom.

The conditions for unworthiness are past. The conditions of worthiness are upon you. This worthiness is your right of passage to the realm of freedom of being within the light of reason.

Gloria Excelsior

Now, how does all of this work for you? How will you begin to see this wealth that is now in front of you and within your experience at this moment in time?

Embedded within your countenance will be many codes to exemplify this beautiful awakening to the understanding of worthiness. These codes, embedded within your DNA, are added strands for this understanding to become the experience of your worth. This strand of worthiness is yours to have and has been manifested for your beautiful countenance. This is your wealth. This is your new determination. This is your reception into worthiness. This new strand of expression is the condition of worthiness that is yours to behold.

It has been given to you by the one and is within the guidelines of universal law declared by the all. This gift provides you with freedom to experience your truth as it manifests within the truth of your worthiness.

We are well pleased with this result. The Gloria and the Lord thy God share this laughter with you as this experience begins to unfold into the light of freedom of being. We thrive, expand, and move within these accepted conditions.

You see, dear ones, we are all one. We all thrive; we all experience; we are light and love. This book six is about the receipt of this light and love. This light and love is a reflection shown through personal worthiness. This worthiness is yours and will always be yours.

Through this evolutionary process, there has been great gain in understanding. This pathway has been opened and supported by many masters who reside on the Earth today. This work has been powerfully led and has strongly impacted the deeds of those who have been able to attend to the teachings given.

Embedded within these teachings has been light filtering through your countenance. This light, filled with love from divine elements, calls to the soul to awaken and to be part of the learning process of desire—the desire to share the light with others to partake in this wisdom of knowing. Through the conditions of these teachings from the masters of light, many processes have been created for the evolutionary pathway of enlightened understanding to unfold into a rebirthing condition. These processes were guided by the Lord thy God and the Gloria who knows.

The Pretender, Called the Shadow

THE SHADOW OF RESISTANCE is a condition of unworthiness. It is another fog that floats and surrounds the truth of self. This shadow of resistance cloaks the truth in resistance. This resistance is a strong denial and destroyer of the true self and is an acceptance of unworthiness. This unworthiness is transparent. It worships the darkness of discontent but pretends to hold reverence for the light. This resistance is a pretender of the truth and presents its nature as the savior of the true self.

This resistance tells stories of worthiness in the form of unworthiness. It creates situations to provide solace through unworthy efforts and misguidance. It is the voice of doom, the voice of fear, and the voice of the challenger of light and love.

This shadow of resistance hides very cleverly. It broods, resists, exhausts, and depletes tenaciously. It reveres a shrinking of the self and provides excuses for actions of intention. This pretender fogs and covers the light that is always available; it cowers in the corner of a darkened room. This room is named unworthiness.

Within this unworthy room, there are many furnishings that provide comfort. These furnishings become familiar and are appointed with gold, silver, and jewels. There are multilayered carpets, chandeliers, and walls that expand and contract at will. Sometimes the room becomes a mansion of wealth where one can reside with great security. Within these walls, there is a sense of worthiness. The twisting of this truth is full and complete. The chandeliers provide false light. The riches of

The Light of Reason

furnishings provide false wealth. The safety of the room becomes a prison of intention. The shadow of resistance to light is complete.

Do you see, dear ones, the story of discontent and the form of unworthiness that comprises denial of the true self—the soul of God?

Now, with this understanding, there is an understanding of your truth. This is not who you are. This is the fog of denial, the fog of resistance, the fog of mistrust, the fog of unforgiving, the fog of the denial of the Lord thy God.

Be aware of this fog. Awareness is the blessing of the Gloria who knows. See this fog for what it is. See this pull for what it is. Challenge this fog with light and love; watch it roll away into wisps of lightening fragments. Watch your countenance change from chains to freedom. Measure your worthiness by observing the lightening of your countenance. Therein will be the observation of freedom, the moving toward the new truth of being.

It is said by many, seeing is believing. What do you see, dear ones?

There is only love.

We are the love. We are the light. May this light shine upon your countenance, and may this lesson unfold with beauty, significance, and honor that is well-deserved through this evolutionary process of your being!

Book Seven

Trust

The Breaking of Chains

BOOK SEVEN BEGINS IN the truth of worth. This is about the truth of trust in the Lord thy God and the truth of endurance.

What is endurance without trust in your divinity? What is endurance without the understanding of personal worthiness in the self and in the other?

With the understanding of this truth and acknowledgement of potential, we can move forward together. Book Seven contains information about the concept of endurance.

Within this quality of endurance will be the growth of potential of all living beings on this planet called the new Earth. This potential of enduring qualities within all needed elements will manifest quickly and easily for the well-being of all living things in this earthly realm. You see, dear ones, this is not a fairy tale. This is your reality within the truth of who you really are. This reality is of your making. This reality is a reflection of your being of light, which manifests real outcomes through service to others. This is your true potential and reflects reality.

Wherefore I say unto you, put down your swords of discontent. Put down your protection, and face your truth with courage, strength, and endurance. This is your call to action. This is your call to express your truth through the reality of enduring qualities.

These enduring qualities can be named. They are known qualities that express worthiness of character. Conditions of strength are met through endurance, which is strength of will within the range of freewill.

There is a memory of containment where one was confined by chains of reaction pulled by the darker elements of existence. These chains diminish the self and deplete being.

These memories provide internal strength and fortitude to witness the breaking of these restrictive bonds. These memories assist you to see the truth of the light of reason, and help reveal the truth of who you really are. This deepening offers a more grateful understanding of the process of divine love.

The quality of endurance is the underpinning for these next qualities to be revealed to exemplify your true, worthy nature. You see, dear ones, the nature of worth flows, widens, and beckons you forward onto your path to divine love. This enlightened place of being is the goal for many on this beautiful, reverential Earth.

Reverence is the next passage one takes when moving along the path of endurance. How does the term reverence reflect or manifest in today's conceptual understanding?

Reverence is a reflection of love and light to all fellow beings on this planet.

Reverence is a passionate understanding of all things as divine elements within the divine plan.

Reverence is the reflection of the truth of all living and non-living things on this planet of desire.

Reverence is the reflection of personal freewill within the framework of love and light.

This is endurance. This is the reflection of enduring qualities.

The next condition of reverence is one of service—the reaching out in service to others in need. Combinations of conditions of service fall within the elements of endurance. Meeting needs of the community flows deeply into the river of desire. This river of desire is an outcome of independence, self-worth, and commitment to the all who reflect compassion for fellow human beings. This action of desire within service elements calls for strength, courage, action, and endurance. Fortitude is also a well-placed term for this understanding.

Endurance is fortitude. It is the action of seeing a condition within a worthiness outcome. The need is seen or witnessed. The outcome is designed. The action is bold, swift, and appropriate. Enduring qualities are established within the guidance of divine love, light, and reverence for the ones receiving this natural flow of loving response from others.

Worthiness is the desire of the true self. To express the outcome of truth within a worthy state, one must demonstrate endurance. This state of endurance exemplifies a deepening condition of self that has never been exposed before. This exposure is the end result of the display of enduring qualities.

Divine Planning

DIVINE PLANNING IS CRITICALLY important to all proposed planning ventures by those who are within the guidelines of service. Within the guidelines of service will be specific unity movements in the planning phases of outreach programs.

The outreach planning phases will be orchestrated by the one who knows. The Gloria will be the initial catalyst for changes manifested through others who will move forward into their service requirements.

How will this work, dear ones? It is a question that moves with the cadence of freewill, desire, endurance, and action within the term of fortitude. The Gloria, who is the Glory, who is the power of the Lord thy God, will orchestrate the unity with a call of desire. This call will be within a manifestation of desire for those who are willing to partake in this adventure of service.

You see, dear ones, all who are ready and willing will witness this call of intention from the Gloria. With this intention comes responsibility—the responsibility of endurance, worthiness, and reverence.

Reverence is the reflection of worthiness. Reverence is the reflection of God, who is the Holy Spirit, who is of the Gloria, who is of the source of all things. Do you see, my loved ones? We are all of the same mold. We are all of Source. We are all unified in this service within the desire for well-being for all, above and below. This service is for a divine purpose. We are of this purpose. We are of this worth. We are of this divine plan.

Gloria Excelsior

Everything that is spoken, heard, and felt is from God, the source, the all, the power, the glory, the Gloria. All attachment to love and light elements of existence is yours to have. Yes, this is your right of passage, your worth, and your intention for being. This is the expression of life with the experience of the divine plan. This, and only this, is the expression of consciousness within life's existence of being. You are within this plan. You are the experience. You are the divinity of expression. You are in receipt of this wealth and are held in deep reverence for this service for the all of existence. This reverence is the expression of your truth, your existence.

We, the Lord thy God and Gloria, are moved by this display of enduring qualities. We are moved by your service of desire. We are well pleased with your nature of being, and we are ready to present your next gift to you for this service of reverence.

Meeting Challenges with Fortitude

THIS GIFT IS IN the name of the Gloria, who serves you with assurance of being. This is the gift of fortitude. Embedded within this understanding are new codes of worthiness. This is another strand connected to DNA particles that will exemplify well-being in the deeper connection of fortitude. We are well pleased with this placement, and this gift truly honors the worthiness of all participating beings on this planet called the new Earth.

Welcome to the golden age of the light of reason, where all challenges will be addressed with fortitude and a willingness to express one's truthfulness through one's freewill nature.

There will be a moment in time when all participants on this planet will be challenged. This moment is of your making and is known to you. In this moment, a calling of service will arise.

This moment in time is clear, precise, and warranted in its outcome. This outcome is the condition of an earthly change in which the orbital outflow will be manifested from this space and time to another directed position within the cosmos of desire.

There is no need to plan for this event. There is only acceptance of this happening as a reality. This change for the Earth is needed for the survival of all who choose to partake in this adventure called the new Earth.

The change of placement for this struggling and dying Earth space is needed for a new infusion of healing dynamic

Gloria Excelsior

intervention to occur. This new space will rejuvenate, revitalize, and renew all aspects of the soils, waters, and air for the wealth of all living entities on this new earthly plane. The connection to all species will be broadened, supported, and renewed. The animal kingdom will be replenished and renewed. There will be a renewal of all life within the ocean for the provision of needed food supply. Many systems will exhibit great productivity for the servicing of the multitudes in need of sustenance. These changes are the necessary adventure of sustainability given for the renewal of wealth within the new Earth.

This pull, which is safe and secure for all is well planned. Upon reading this page, many will have questions. In that time and moment, those questions will be considered with respect and answered by the one called Gloria. Pay attention to your inner guidance. It is your right to ask questions and to consider the response. It is your right to make decisions about your acceptance or rejection of this new adventure. It is your right to move through your freewill into the personal knowing of an appropriate outcome for your development.

These questions will give you the impetus to express your worthiness and to move toward the true nature of your being. Truth will begin to express a desire that will call for a decision. This is the ultimate expression of freewill, my loves. The freewill is of your own making. This freewill is of your worthiness and of your truthful nature. This is your gift and always has been your freedom to be within your truth. This truth is held in high reverence and is respected through universal law.

The Adventure

Let's continue with this information. We, the consortium who comprise the masters of light, are connected to you through the knowledge we are expressing on this page of text. The challenges you are facing are replete with new conditions. These new conditions are held with high reverence and are well-respected. We, the masters, are channeling this conversation through the Gloria, who is the Lord thy God, who is the Source, the all.

We, the masters, have lived, breathed, had families, and experienced much on this Earth through many lifetimes; we have watched you make choices that became part of the reality that you are experiencing today. Through these choices, actions have followed. These actions have held endurance and reverence and have manifested many outcomes. These outcomes have served you well in maintaining the status of human existence.

Now it is time for a change, for this existence is finished. This planet, in this space, cannot survive the stresses upon it. This planet, as we know it, is dying. No interventions can renew or save it.

There is no recrimination, no judgment of the end result. There is no plaintive cry of remorse, for the pathway of choice is honored through freewill and reverence according to universal law.

All choices have been appropriate.

All choices have been within worthiness outcomes.

All outcomes have been within experience.

All experiences are held in ordained reverence.

How can we declare this? Do you not know who you are? You are the experience; you are the masters who have walked upon this Earth. You are the divine ones who play in the fields. You are the extraordinary outcome of all the experiences since the beginning of time. You are the seed of God lighting the way. You are the seed of God who experiences, develops knowing, and moves through challenges and intentions.

We, the masters, are telling you something very important. It is time to listen very closely. We, the consortium of masters, are part of the moving team for this new Earth experience. This team of potential power moves together as a unit. Yes, we are unified as one. With this understanding, we want to make this clear.

Through the ages, we have presented to you on this Earth many teachings. These teachings have, in many respects, been guiding principles for your daily life; they have been honored through the ages. They have impacted your life, and you have applied these teachings according to your worthiness experiences.

Within these teachings, there has always been the understanding of freewill about how you interpret and integrate these teachings into your countenance. Be still with this understanding. Do you see how personal or collective interpretations through worthiness begin to change these teachings?

We, the masters of light and love, say this to you. We are one. We have always been one. We live as one. There has only been one.

How can this be, you say? How can this not be?

We have come to you in many forms throughout the ages. We have pushed you forward many times, helping you find your rightful path along the experiential road. This path is the reflection of your truth. The finding of your truth has only been

The Light of Reason

the demarcation of reality—the reality of discovering your true identity and the truth of your higher self, which is your soul of God.

What an adventure! Do you see? Through the ages, you have been pulled forward into discovering stages of who you really are within the truth of the cosmos of desire. You are a child of God. You are the planted seed. You are the experience, as you live through the experience, to experience your truth through your discovery and freewill. This pull is complete. The pull to your evolutionary destiny on this old Earth is complete.

There is no division of self. There is only experience within the self of understanding.

The self manifests into many seeds, and through these seeds, there is growth. Through this growth, everything expresses perfection within the experience, for all seeds are of God, Source, and the all. All expresses through these seeds of beauty, wealth, and freewill.

Now it is appropriate to discuss the next pull for this new evolutionary pathway to unfold. We, the masters of light and love, hold this potential, along with Gloria, who is the Lord thy God, Source, the all, to claim a new space for this Earth. This service will be done in the name of all universal elements.

Many manifestations have occurred on this Earth over many lifetimes. Yes, you call them miracles. These miracles or manifestations are ordained and appropriate through universal law. The pull for the new location of Earth has been decreed by universal law. We, the masters of light, are part of this controlled movement of desire.

Gloria Excelsior

You see, dear ones, this pull will be a new making of this dying Earth. This will be the rejuvenation for all on this new planet of desire. The changes of the dynamics will be monitored by the all. As the Earth is pulled, it will be within manifestations of blessings. These blessings will be in the form of safety and security for all on this planet of movement. There will be a shifting of the axis. There will be a stretching of day and night observations, and there will be a stabilizing of weather patterns to bring comfort to all who reside in this new venture in time and space.

We, the masters, are well pleased with this next pull of evolutionary growth. We are the potential, the light, and the reason for being. We are one with the Gloria who reflects the age of light of reason, which is the new evolutionary stage for all to experience.

We are well pleased.

Afterword

WE, THE PRESENT AVATARS, who are on this Earth, speak to you directly. We are honored to be of the house of nirvana. Since our arrival we have brought forth many gifts to this planet. Embedded within these gifts is the gift of truth and forgiveness. Within truth and forgiveness we have brought forth Gloria through manifestation of being. She is our delight. She is our wealth. She is our understanding.

Do you see dear ones? We are all from the same spark of divinity and of the divine soul.

We exist today and have been living on this Earth in a very sacred and sanctified place called the Oneness University. We have created this space specifically for the coming of the glory who is the Gloria.

This sacred place has much history and is full of delight. Many masters have visited through this living entity which is a structure within the university grounds. This structure has received many seekers from around the world who have moved through these sacred spaces.

Through this movement of peoples who have come to stay for short or longer periods of time, a special entity has appeared to us in the name of Gloria. She is bonded to this university along with all masters of light and love who have entered through these doors.

Our role, as avatars has been given a specific mandate by all divine elements. We have come to this Earth to give you Gloria.

She is the one that is being given to you with our love and gratitude.

We have supported her, provided guidance, moved her to remembering her role as an avatar, and now our job is complete.

This university of wealth and wellbeing has served its initial purpose: To bring forth Gloria who reigns supreme from the house of nirvana.

We are leaving for the house of completion where we will be honored and revered for this immense service and hold much gratitude to all peoples who have moved with us in the name of Sri Amma Bhagavan. All who follow understand the truth. This truth is of oneness, without borders, without nationality, without religious affiliations. We have always represented, through the house of nirvana, universal law and all the respect of diversity that each law demands.

We are pleased with our vision. We are pleased with our loved ones who have experienced this pleasure of moving through the states of awakening to awakened and beyond. We are grateful.

Above all we are grateful to the Gloria, our sister, who will carry on this beginning of using the Oneness University for learning, but will also extend the vision to encompass the wealth that she brings from this house called nirvana.

We have agreed that there will be a merging of Sri Amma Bhagavan, Gloria Excelsior, the Lord thy God, Masters, and all universal elements to form a strong front in strengthening all further manifestations for this new vision that is required for the survival of the new Earth.

With this new intent, we welcome the Gloria to the university where she will sometimes live. We are well pleased and celebrate this coming event with light and love.

Glossary

All	existence of being within the universal framework of knowing
Avatar	descent of a deity in the physical form
Awaken	spring into being or rouse from an unconscious state
Awakened state	tapping into the universal field of intelligence through conscious awareness
Being	the true self, who is the seed of God
Bliss	rapture within consciousness
Challenges	the experience of fear
Compassion	passion for others within their choice of action
Cosmos of reason	the well-ordered whole of universal intelligence
Counterpoint	point against point; precursor to meeting the expressed challenge or not
Darkness	the experience of fear
Divine intelligence	the expression of loving delight for the natural evolution for all

Divinity	the godhead
Duality	a structure of the mind creating opposites within the experience
Elements	the basic premise for life itself
Existence	the conscious desire to create through the universal field of knowing
Fortitude	maintaining personal integrity in the midst of hardship
Freewill	the highly honored right choice of all revered beings under universal law
Golden age	a period of success
House of nirvana	A place of divinity and union
Intention	the power of now within the sanctified process of agreement through all levels of collective consciousness
In utero	the state of the embryo or fetus in the womb
Light	divine love elements
Manifestations	the materialization or proof of a gift of grace from divine intention sometimes called miracles
Masters	divinity of light and love who are one
Neutrality	no thing to judge or rate

New world order	the orderly fashioning of a people's forum under universal law of agreement
Notation	numbers too big or too small to be conventionally written in decimal form (scientific notation)
Now	not of linear time; in the presence of conscious awareness
One	the expression of living and non-living things through form
Plane of fortitude	the quest for enlightenment
Power and the glory	the merging of the masculine and feminine divine into one
Receipt	recognition of grace from divine elements
Redemption	forgiveness for the self and for others
Resistance	fear, forming a pattern of darkness, distancing the self from healing light factors
Savior	the protector offering forgiveness and guidance within saving grace elements
Salvation	conditions of worthiness that are given
Self	the soul, which is representative of all universal potential of light and love

Synergy	working together
Tunnel of awareness	the field that holds light and dark elements of discovery
Unit	collective consciousness moves through one within the all
Wealth	worthiness, blessings, and grace exemplify a richness of being within the field of universal consciousness
Will	a highly respected creative process within the choice and experience of Being
Witnessing	becoming aware of inner thoughts, emotions, and deeds, as seen through a lens of clarity

CPSIA information can be obtained at www.ICGtesting.com
Printed in the USA
LVOW06s0958201114

414562LV00001B/11/P

9 781452 523637